I0505321

Contents

About the author & this book 3

Chapter 1: Strategy and Planning 7

Chapter 2: Social media profiles 10

Chapter 3: Your website 22

Chapter 4: Content 29

Chapter 5: Content Creation 47

Chapter 6: Smart Content Tactics 54

Chapter 7: Instagram 67

Chapter 8: Twitter 71

Chapter 9: LinkedIn 81

Chapter 10: Facebook 90

Chapter 11: Pinterest 102

Chapter 12: TikTok 107

Chapter 13: Blogging 111

Chapter 14: Messaging Apps 114

Chapter 15: Other Platforms 116

Chapter 16: Prospecting 123

Chapter 17: Building Trust 145

Chapter 18: Running Campaigns 149

Chapter 19: Time Saving Tips 155

Chapter 20: The Integrated Approach 160

Chapter 21: Analyse and improve 166

Chapter 22: Sharpening the saw 179

Chapter 23: Conclusion 182

Chapter 24: Bonus Materials! 184

About the author & this book

About the author

Hi, and welcome to my book on how to use social media to grow your business. I have poured my 25 years of sales and marketing experience (including over 11 years supporting over 200 businesses on social media) into this book.

Before you read on, here's a quick overview of me, and what to expect from this book.

I have successfully run a digital marketing business since 2011, serving customers and posting content to more than 100,000 fans on a regular basis.

My approach to social media is to ensure that businesses generate results from the efforts and investment that they make. The key focus for businesses is to ensure that they not only increase their presence online, but also succeed in achieving a solid return on investment (ROI).

I have a vast experience in a range of platforms including Twitter, Facebook, Pinterest, Instagram and LinkedIn.

I'm also passionate about languages and new technologies, which in a way fit in with social media where the technology and practices are changing rapidly.

** NOTE ** This book has been updated in 2022 to reflect changes in social media and the ways platforms such as Instagram, LinkedIn or TikTok work.

Welcome to my must-have book on social media for business. If you want to generate more business and grow your brand online then this book will help.

I have designed and written this book to make your social media activities as easy as possible, while getting the best results.

The book contains 150 quick and easy ways to make your social media more effective, and each activity should take a maximum of 20 minutes to do (and in many cases just a few seconds!) - and they will make a huge difference to the way you approach social media - and the success you achieve.

In some cases, activities such as interacting on social media can or should be done on a daily basis. The activity might take 10 or 20 minutes to do but on a regular basis, rather than as a one-off.

If you have started using social media but are not sure how to make it work for your business, then this book is perfect for you. This book is for people with knowledge of social media ranging from the beginner who has been using social media for a few months through to the expert who needs more ideas and inspiration to achieve success.

Useful as an ongoing reference

#BOOSTMYBUSINESS has been designed so that you can continue to use it as a reference, allowing you to refer to individual sections when you need to.

If you are working on your website development for example, then you can refer to the website section with a small list of highly effective activities regarding your website and social media.

I fully recommend that you read through this book first from front to back before then keeping it close at hand to refer to when you need to.

Please note that some of the 150 ways might be similar. This is because some activities work differently on social media and some practices might relate to multiple sections such as your website or, for example, prospecting. Despite the title of this book, I have also included MORE than 150 ways to make sure you get great value out of this book.

Social media is moving fast, and the book covers the latest social media platforms that will give you the best results.

At the beginning of the book, we will cover the basics including the effective set up of social media profiles, before we go through sales generations tactics such as content marketing and prospecting.

Feel free to connect

Before we get in to chapter 1, you are welcome to follow me on social media for more great tips and the latest updates.

You can connect with me on a whole range of social media platforms from TikTok and Twitter to LinkedIn, Facebook and Instagram.

Below are the links for a selection of my profiles as well as a link to the website for Think Twice Marketing, the business which I run:

Twitter: @Darrenhignett
(or www.Twitter.com/darrenhignett)

TikTok: @Darrenhignett
(or https://www.tiktok.com/@darrenhignett)

LinkedIn:
https://www.linkedin.com/in/darrenhignett

Facebook: https://www.facebook.com/ThinkTwiceMarketingUK

Instagram: Darren_hignett
https://www.instagram.com/darren_hignett

The Think Twice Marketing website:
https://www.thinktwicemarketing.com

Chapter 1: Strategy and Planning

As you start to formulate your plans, it's important to make sure you have a clear social media marketing strategy. This chapter covers some important considerations that you should have worked out by now.

If you haven't, then now is the time to make sure you have the right plans in place!

1. Be clear on who your target audience is

Any activity you do should always bear in mind that you need to find the right people who want to buy from you.

There is no point interacting on Instagram or LinkedIn with people who are very unlikely to buy from you.

It might be fun interacting with them but finding an hour later that you have interacted with lots of people that aren't your target audience can be a huge waste of time.

Be clear on who your target audience is and where they 'hang out' before you put time aside to interact.

I love the phrase 'deadlines get things done'. If you randomly do some prospecting when you find a bit of time, then you are likely to get distracted by other things going on around you and other activities on your to-do list but if you

set targets and include a deadline then this will help you to focus.

If LinkedIn, for example, is the perfect platform for you to prospect on, then set a target to find 5 or 10 potential customers every day.

The target could be based on how many people you invite to become a connection, how many become connections or how many you interact with on posts, articles, and messages.

The targets and how high they are will depend on you and your type of business. The important thing is to have targets that work for you and that keep you focused on growing sales.

You might have heard of the term SMART goals (goals that are Specific, Measurable, Attainable, Relevant and Time-based).

Having goals that motivate you and are realistic and can be measured are important to them leading to the right results.

If you want to find out more about SMART goals and objectives, then just Google search for SMART goals.

I don't want to be too promotional in this book, and I hope you don't mind, but I also have a book called Setting Goals that Get Results.

If you want to take your goal setting and achievements to the next level, then you might want to grab a copy of this book for your next read.

3. Create a prospect daily, content weekly plan

We have talked about prospecting on a daily basis and using a template to outline what activities you will do.

When it comes to an overall plan, I strongly recommend prospecting daily but planning content on a weekly basis.

If you try to plan content on a daily basis, then it can be time consuming, and you will quickly find that the day has gone by while you play around with picture or video editing and so on.

Planning content monthly is great, but it requires a lot of work in one go – and you might prefer to do this.

However, I prefer weekly planning as it's more manageable and strikes the right balance between being efficient and having time put to one side to focus on content creation and scheduling.

Chapter 2: Social media profiles

In later chapters we will talk about prospecting to find customers as well as doing effective marketing campaigns but before that, it is important to get the fundamentals of a social media profile right.

If you have just recently set up your social media profile, then the most important thing to do first is make sure your profiles look great and are attention grabbing!

Even if you have already been using social media for a while, take a look through the sections below and make sure your profiles are set up for impact.

4. Go Visual with great bio images

You know the saying "Image is everything"? Well, it isn't quite everything but if you don't have images on your social media profiles then don't read the rest of this chapter until you have.

In fact, do not just have images... have good images, it's very important.

When a customer visits your profile, the first thing they will see are the images. If they are not appropriate or don't convey the right message, then it's possible you have lost the customer already!

Follow the steps below to make sure images are working for you.

Have an image!

This sounds very basic, yet so many people don't do this. Would you buy a second-hand car on a website if there was no image? I certainly wouldn't. In fact, I would think there was something wrong with it. The same applies on social media.

A good quality image of you or your business logo is important, but it if you don't have images that you are completely happy with then at least having a basic image is better than having no image at all.

You can use tools such as Canva (www.canva.com) to resize your images. Most social media platforms require images to be a set width and height, and Canva has templates you can select depending on if the image is to be used for a LinkedIn, Facebook, or some other background.

Set the avatar image as a brand logo or a picture of you

When setting up a business page on Google or Facebook use a branded logo as your avatar (or thumbnail) image. This is also the same for a LinkedIn company page (although your own personal profile should always be an image of you!).

For Twitter and Pinterest, there are good reasons for having a picture of you as a profile image rather than a brand - but then there are also good reasons why your brand image should be used.

A picture of you is more likely to get interactions at a personal level as people will associate their interactions with the person in the image.

However, if your company has more than one person managing your company Twitter account then using a brand image is better. Added to this, a brand logo conveys an overall appearance that your company is bigger than just one person.

Whichever option you decide, do NOT present your profile with an action shot that is blurred and difficult to see clearly.

Make background images suggestive in terms of the services you offer

The background image is the largest and the first image someone will see when viewing your profile. The most effective images are the ones which are suggestive of what services (and benefits) you provide.

I have seen some background images which show the team at the company (all with smiling faces and smartly dressed, ready to serve their customers).

This is good and gives a human element to the profile. It doesn't, however, say anything about what the company does.

Remember, when people look at a social media profile (just like opening the page of a newspaper) the first thing they will look at is the background image and the profile image. An image of four or five team members might look personal, but it can quickly lose the attention of a prospective customer and they will go away not knowing what you offer.

Here are some ideas of background images for various types of businesses:

- A health nutritionist might use a background image of people who are smiling, happy and enjoying themselves with a positive quote included, thus demonstrating a healthy lifestyle.
- A restaurant can appeal to customers by showing people inside the restaurant eating a fantastic meal. This action shot helps people to visualise themselves in the restaurant having a great time and enjoying good food.
- A tour operator may use a picture of people on holiday having a great time. Not only does this image suggest that the company provides holidays but again, it appeals to people's emotions by demonstrating the benefits of having a great holiday. This is much more effective than an image of the inside of a booking office.

Don't forget – "A picture says a thousand words"! The right picture for a restaurant with people enjoying their food in a great atmosphere will help attract more clients before they have even started to look at your posts or engage with you.

After a first-time visitor has viewed the images and title on your social media profile, the next thing they will do is read your bio. The bio must convey what you offer and the key benefit you offer in a small amount of space.

Added to this, the challenge is also to word the bio so that when people read it, they want to follow you or like your page. Here are some important points to check:

Make sure your bio says what you or what you offer

This is another one of those 'stating the obvious' activities that often doesn't get done correctly. A hotel, for example, may think it's okay to have a description that says, "serving customers", but what does this really say? A better bio would include what they are serving customers with locally and how long they have been doing it.

If they cater for weddings or major events that should be included. If their speciality is catering for families, then that could be included. A better bio might read: "serving customers with wedding events locally for over 30 years".

Make sure your bio conveys a strong benefit or your unique selling point

As well as the bio explaining what you offer, make sure to get across at least one major benefit. In the hotel example above, mentioning that the hotel has been serving people locally for over 30 years helps to build trust that the hotel is well established and understands the local market. A restaurant may use similar wording to build trust by saying "serving award winning food locally for over 30 years".

The use of the term "award-winning" will surely attract customers who want to try out the experience of a restaurant that is award-winning!

Getting the message right in your bio is important and it's worth testing your bio out on friends and colleagues to see what they think. You may even want to use the services of a copywriter who is familiar with using words that have a higher impact (known as power words).

Power words are key!

When writing your bio, think about power words. These are words that influence people's thinking and perception.

Power words such as delicious, easy, guaranteed results or award-winning can mean the difference between average and awesome sales. If you support businesses to help them grow then say that you have been SUCCESFULLY supporting businesses, helping them to grow. The word success or successfully in your description increases the chances of somebody wanting to buy from you.

Power words play a vital role in your bio as well as in content that you post on social media, wording you use in email marketing campaigns and on your website.

If you are not familiar with power words or would like to learn more then I highly recommend a blog by Buffer which gives 189 great power words that you can use for better results (or should that be amazing, revolutionary, even remarkable results? – you get the idea!).

The Big List of 189 Words That Convert by Buffer:

https://blog.bufferapp.com/words-and-phrases-that-convert-ultimate-list

Consider the personal element in your bio

If your bio has a personal, fun or light-hearted element then it increases the chances that people will take an interest in you on social media – and want to interact! You don't have to include a personal element, but it will increase the possibility of higher interactions and results, a bit like power words.

Once you have written your bio, I suggest passing it by work colleagues or friends to see what they think. If you really aren't sure if you have the right wording and you don't feel comfortable with it then don't publish it straight away.

Save it as a draft in a word document and leave it for 24 hours. Revisit what you have written the next day when the mind is fresh, and you have a different perspective.

Have a call to action in your bio

Your profile picture and bio might be the first thing a prospect sees of you on social media. It is also what a lot of potential customers will check before deciding if they should buy from you. Having a call to action such as offering a FREE consultation, a FREE download or simply using words such as 'visit our website now to get the latest stuff' will help entice potential customers to take action.

Use the right keywords – especially on LinkedIn

If you want to be found on social media (and why wouldn't you?) then having the right keywords in your personal bio and general information sections is important.

This is especially true on LinkedIn where people will search for companies and professional contacts. Whereas Twitter and Pinterest have very little space for you to explain what you do, the benefits and the skills that you offer, LinkedIn is different.

There is ample opportunity to include this information in a way that gets you found whilst at the same time showing off your talents to people once they are reading your profile.

Spend 10 minutes just going through your LinkedIn profile to make sure you have the necessary words in your summary and endorsements that you think people are searching for.

Other parts of your bio

Having a full bio with plenty of detail looks a lot more professional but many of these different areas to fill in are nice to have and possibly less relevant in bringing in new business.

Depending on which social media platform you are using, you will be presented with other fields to fill in that can be visible by your audience.

The two important fields which are present on most platforms is the location field and the URL (where you can add your website).

We will focus on these below:

Add your location

When adding your location make sure to set it according to your target market. If you are a brand you may want to have your location as UK or global for example, but a restaurant or shop should be more specific by mentioning the town.

It's important to add your location so that you can be found by the right people.

There may be companies out there with a similar name to yours but on a different continent altogether! If you don't have a location, then you risk getting followers that actually have no interest in you.

If I am looking for dentists in Portsmouth, then your profile is more likely to appear in search results if your location is set up correctly as 'Portsmouth'.

You may also want to clarify your location in certain circumstances. If your location is a town such as Andover, Birmingham or Whitchurch then you might be based in the USA, UK or (as in the example of Whitchurch) based in one of many locations across the UK.

If this is the case, add the country to your location as well. Companies set up in New York or London certainly need not worry about this!

Add your URL

Getting found on social media is a great start – but only the start. When somebody has looked at your profile and is interested in your services then they will want to know more.

Not having a web link to your website is a fundamental error that can mean the difference between having 200 visitors making enquiries and 200 visitors who don't know how to get in touch with you - and they won't!

Consider having your URL point to a specific landing page rather than your homepage. If you are an online retailer, you may point directly to your online shop for greater results.

A great way to generate leads on your website is also to have a URL on social media pointing visitors to a page with a lead capture form. With one click from your profile they can then complete the form and get in touch.

If you use Google analytics then you can track how many people are visiting your website but if this is something that you don't do, consider using a URL shortener such as through Hootsuite or a bit.ly to create a shortened URL.

You can then track the number of clicks on the link in your profile. This helps to understand how effective your profile is at converting views to clicks.

Note: More than 70% of people use mobile devices to access social media. Make sure your URL points to a mobile friendly page on your site and that your site is mobile friendly!

Chapter 3: Your website

It's easy to spend days endlessly modifying your website in order to make it perfect when the reality is that many of the activities you do or words and images you add don't bring in business. This isn't an exaggeration!

Just because your website looks beautiful does not mean you will attract and convert opportunities. Just because it is easy to navigate doesn't mean that customers will buy from you.

A knowledgeable web company will tell you that visitors are typically on a website for less than 3 minutes. In some cases, the average site visit can be as low as 30 to 60 seconds after which time a prospective client could be lost forever.

Imagine this, you have spent good money on Pay Per Click, SEO (Search Engine Optimisation) or some other form of marketing activity to get people to your website and within seconds they are gone... forever. There are two simple ways to keep the customer 'connected' with you.

Firstly, you could add a contact form to capture their details for re-establishing contact. Usually, most businesses use the email address to start an email marketing campaign to the website visitor but there are other options.

Secondly, by simply adding social media icons to your website, you are offering customers who on are not yet ready to buy the opportunity to stay in contact with you.

Here are some quick and easy ways to make your website more effective from a social media perspective (note: we are not talking about overall web design here, capture forms or email marketing).

6. Invite people to connect on social media from your website

Make sure to include the option for visitors to your website to be able to connect with you on social media. You should include the ability to connect to all social media platforms that you use, not just Facebook or Twitter for example. Make sure to include the ability to connect from every page of your website.

Platforms such as Twitter, Facebook and Pinterest allow you to create icons or widgets which include the ability for visitors to quickly connect with you.

Make sure to use the official logos. Using the logo means people know what they are connecting to rather than just words with an embedded URL that says, "click here to like us on Facebook".

When using the widgets, you can also customise them to suit the layout and theme of your website. The level of customisation is a little bit limited, but you can still make some basic changes such as background or text colour and size of the widget on Twitter.

7. Use the share button to spread awareness of your website content

If you have pages with news releases, embedded blogs or other useful information then make sure to include the share widgets; allowing readers to share useful information from your website onto their Twitter or Facebook newsfeed.

These widgets are widely available and should take only 5 to 10 minutes to install on your website. Once they are installed, your website visitors will start marketing your website for you!

8. Install the Facebook Pixel code on your website.

Facebook pixel code is a small snippet of code from Facebook that you can add to your website. Facebook is then able to track visitors who visit your website that are also logged into Facebook.

The social media platform is then able to do some pretty smart stuff such as understand the type of people who visit your website and build up a profile of what your target audience looks like.

Facebook pixel code is ideally for use with Facebook Ads, which we will cover later on, but even if you don't plan on doing any ads in the short-term future, it's work implementing this code.

In order to build up data on your audience so that you can target them better, the code needs to be on your site for as long as possible. If you decide to use Facebook Ads 6 or even 12 months later then Facebook will have the data to be able to target the right people and increase the chances of getting the results you want.

9. Integrate your blog activity with your website

There are many benefits of integrating blogging with social media. By closely linking your blog to your website, you are bringing social media and web search closer together.

A good blog that is optimised for SEO will attract customers searching on Google. Imagine someone searching for how to do something that you have written a blog on. Your blog appears in the Google search and the user clicks on your blog to read it.

After reading the article they were looking for they can then click through to your website for more information about your business. Trust has also been gained that you clearly know what you are talking about as well.

On the flipside, visitors to your website are more likely to stay on your site for longer and become familiar with your brand. They may click through to your blog, read some of your content and either decide to share it or connect with you on social media. You can also use the blog to redirect readers back to relevant areas on your website!

The great thing about Pinterest is that it is highly visual. If you are regularly pinning on the social media platform, then you can let visitors to your website directly see your product (or other) images that you have posted on Pinterest.

This live feed also reduces the need to constantly update your website with fresh images.

Here are some examples where this can be used:

A bakery can post images of fresh cakes including seasonal items such as hot cross buns at Easter, wedding cakes in the summer and possibly their great range of Christmas goodies. That should entice customers – especially if delicious products are posted around lunch time!

A photographer can post examples of recently taken work with a live feed appearing on the website. This could include work done for customers as well as seasonal images taken from spring and summer through to winter.

Note: According to research done in 2013 by HelloSociety, 88% of people surveyed went on to purchase a product that they had re-pinned on Pinterest. The ability to add links on Pinterest is very powerful. Another great reason to have a live feed of your products on your website.

11. Use Social Sign-In

One of the biggest reasons that people abandon a shopping cart online is frustration when having to register. Many people simply do not like having to provide so much information and give up when it becomes too much hassle.

A great way to overcome this is by using a company such as SeatID to implement social sign in. This basically means that the user can register with your website using their Facebook or other social media account.

This can reduce the time it takes to sign up on your website from minutes to seconds while increasing the number of people who will sign up!

There are also other clever things you can do such as prompt users to Like your Facebook page when signing in to grow your social media profile further. Creating and setting this up shouldn't be a lot of time and effort but there may be ongoing costs involved.

12. Use RSS feeds and pictures for your blog posts

A lot of people make the mistake when writing blog posts that they don't include a header image. As well as helping a blog post to look nice, a header image also helps when posting a blog post on social media.

Depending on who you host your site with and your settings, platforms such as Twitter and LinkedIn should generate a thumbnail in your social media posts using your header image - and not having a header image can make the social media post look unprofessional or unattractive.

LinkedIn and Facebook are both good at generating thumbnails when you add a url to a post. Thumbnails are highly effective as they are large areas that anyone can click on and be taken immediately to website or blog post that you have included. Twitter sometimes doesn't generate thumbnails and you can overcome this by creating what's called Twitter Cards, but this can be a tricky process.

Even if you don't manage to have thumbnails working for Twitter, the header image will appear in some scheduling apps such as Buffer with the option to use that instead.

If you can't create a great looking thumbnail then you can, at least, add a highly visual image instead.

Having a header image is useful not just when you post on social media. Your target audience might like your blog posts and decide post them on their social media profiles as well.

Chapter 4: Content

"Social media is called social media for a reason. It lends itself to sharing rather than horn-tooting."
~ Margaret Atwood

Wherever you look for advice on social media, you always get feedback that content is king. If your content isn't good enough, you won't succeed.

To a certain extent that is true. If your content sucks then followers will leave you, in pursuit of more interesting, exciting, engaging (or whatever superlative you can think of) content.

If your content is great, it doesn't necessarily guarantee you will get sales, but it does increase your presence online.

Think of this for example: You do a post of high value to your 500 followers. A follower on Twitter, who is also a customer of yours, retweets it to their 500 friends. Two of their followers then retweet to their 200 followers.

And this goes on... So far, the number of potential people that have seen your post is 1,400 (your 500 followers plus your customers 500 followers plus the 200 followers each of the other two profiles the retweeted).

A well-designed post to raise awareness of your company, and its services can instantly reach a large audience very quickly.

By the way – I talk above about posting content of high value, but this does not always have to be tips or advice related. Posting something funny or highly 'social' is also good, providing it fits in with your overall branding and image.

There are lots of posts on social media with cuddly cats, and this is the number one thing that gets interactions on social media!

I should point out at this stage that although content is important, don't rely on it as the sole source for finding business and getting results. In my blog 'Content is Not King' I talk about the importance of other elements of social media such as lead generation and using Ads campaigns to generate sales.

These other elements are covered later in the book and must be used in conjunction with great content.

Here is the link to the blog. I strongly recommend having a read:

https://darrenhignett.blogspot.com/2015/04/content-is-not-king.html

I'm not going to go through content styles for different social media platforms in this chapter. That's for another book! You are, however, welcome to get in contact to discuss this further.

Later on, we will cover some great ways to make your social media posts highly effective. Before, that, it's important to have a content strategy and the next two tactics are focused on how to develop the right content approach.

13. Use the ATM approach to generating sales

ATM stands for Attract – Teach – Monetise and the right content marketing strategy is part of this approach.

The way it works is very simple. You attract your target audience to your brand with great content (whether that's your LinkedIn or Instagram profile or to your website and blog posts).

Once you have the attention of your target audience, you educate or teach them with content that's high value. This helps to build trust and brand loyalty.

When your potential customer trusts your brand and understands how you can address their needs or pain points, you then monetise – or, in other words, generate the sale.

Let's take a couple of examples.

A business coach might use LinkedIn and Twitter to attract business owners and send them to their blog posts. Those blog posts provide high value content on topics such as how to set goals correctly, the benefits of delegating when scaling up a business and so on.

All of this content adds value to the business owner and while adding huge value to them, it also subtly sells the need for them to have coaching support.

A car mechanic might post content with winter car care tips, how to check the air pressure and tread on their tyres and so on.

All of these tips help the driver to look after their car, as well as their safety – and when it comes to needing professional support, they are more likely to react to that social media post that offers 10% off a winter service.

There are many ways that you can use the ATM or attract, teach, monetise model – and it works better when social media content is used in conjunction with a lead generation process such as offering a free eBook on a landing page website.

14. Use the right balance of promotional content

Nobody likes being sold to, but if you don't promote your services then how will people ever buy from you?

There are plenty of clever ways that you can overcome this, which we will cover later in this book.

In reality, your target audience doesn't mind seeing a promotional post from, just not all of the time.

If you use the ATM model (mentioned earlier) then potential customers who you have built trust with are more likely to accept – and respond to – promotional posts.

Another great strategy to use is the 3:1 ratio. For every 3 posts that add value or that are highly engaging, have one promotional post.

Doing it this way, ensures that you have a strong focus on providing valuable content to your growing target audience while not forgetting to occasionally prompt your potential customers toward buying from you.

There might be times when you don't use the 3:1 ratio. If, for example, you are running a competition, or a limited time offer then you might want to increase the number of posts to do a countdown – such as 3 days to go…. 2 days to go etc.

In this instance, that's fine assuming that you have built up a healthy deposit of trust with your audience who are more likely to love the competition or offer that you are running.

Let's now focus more on the types of content that you post and what's included in them.

Nowadays, social media is the easiest place to go to find something. ~ David Nail

Earlier on I mentioned how powerful Google is as a search engine. This is true, but there are lots of people who use social media to search for things.

I have presented numerous training courses over the years and remember presenting a training once on social media in which I briefly touched on YouTube and how this was growing in popularity. I remember making a comment about how people love to search for things on YouTube.

I wasn't expecting much response but was amazed when one of the attendees piped up and said that they had used YouTube the other day to find out how to cook something.

Straight after that, somebody then pointed out that they had bought a new pushchair and rather than reading the manual, they had searched on YouTube for how to collapse a particular brand of pushchair to put it into a car.

Let's think about that for a minute. Rather than open a cookbook or read a manual, somebody had gone onto a social media platform and searched instead.

Now we all know that we don't read manuals unless we have to, but this shows how social media is making it easier for us in our busy everyday lives to find what we want.

The importance of using hashtags vary depending on the social media platform but should certainly be used on Twitter, LinkedIn, Instagram and Pinterest. Here are some examples of how searchable hashtags can be used:

A company that provides coaching or management for CEOs and business managers may post top tips on Twitter using #leadership.

A business owner follows a business management style magazine on Twitter (Forbes or Harvard business School for example).

The magazine posts a tweet using #leadership. When the business owner clicks on the #leadership, he will see all the tweets that have used that hashtag, amongst which, there is a chance that he will see the post from the company providing coaching.

The business owner may decide to react to that tweet including clicking a link or following that company (a great way to start a long-term relationship!).

16. Join hashtag conversations

This is more relevant to Twitter than any other platform. When there is a major event on such as a World Cup or exhibition, some bright spark invents a hashtag that can be used.

By logging onto Twitter and clicking on the hashtag, you can easily join the conversation. So, you are probably wondering: why would that be of benefit to my business?

Well, imagine that you sell merchandise such as football kits. You may promote your services and interact with customers using #Worldcup2018 (yes, I am aware this is too late to users but surely #Worldcup2022 is not too far away?).

Similarly, if you are attending an exhibition on displays for retail, where potential customers will visit and there is a conversation around the hashtag #VMDS2022 then you can write a post using this hashtag.

Your potential customers who are also on Twitter will see your post and can join in the conversation.

Just make sure the content is good and worthwhile! You may want to interact with what other people have posted. If a potential supplier has posted the following tweet:

Looking forward to #VMDS2022. Just booked our tickets!

You may want to reply to that and suggest meeting up or just reply with a very generic response stating that it promises to be a good show.

Note: you may also want to add this contact to a list and even follow them. We will go through lists and prospecting later.

Done professionally, inspirational quotes and light-humour and fun can increase engagement and grow your followers and customers.

Here are some ideas to help you:

Posting a famous quote

As a social media expert, I find one of the most time-consuming activities is finding great content regularly.

Making a post with a famous quote is quick and easy to do, and since everybody loves a famous quote, the chances of your post being shared are very high.

There are plenty of websites with quotes. A good one to use is www.brainyquote.com. The easiest way to find good quotes is to go to Google and simply type "quotes about..." And include what you are looking for.

For example, if you are a gym, you may type in "quotes about health".

Your post will be more effective if it is visual, but obviously this does take longer to do. Visual quotes are always worth the extra effort, but if you are posting famous quotes several times a week then clearly there is a trade-off between the time spent designing a good visual post and the return you will get back.

Top tip: On Twitter, use #GreatQuote or #Quotes to increase the chances of your post being found.

For Instagram there are lots of hashtags you can chose from. Here are 25 top trending hashtags you can use when posting an inspirational or motivational quote:

#quotestoliveby #greatquotes #quotes #quotesoftheweek #inspirationalquotes #quote #motivationalquotes #quotesoftheday #quotestoremember #quotesandsayings #quotestoinspire #quotestags #quotes 🖤 #quotesdaily #quoteoftheweek #quoteoftheday #inspiration #powerfulquotes #amazingquotes #successquotes #successquotes #instagood #instaquotes #quotestagram #quotesofinstagram

Add fun to your posts (cats included)

Cats (and babies) always get great interactions on social media, but you shouldn't make every single post about cats! Having said that, the reason cats are so popular on social media is because it adds a fun element to the content.

It's great having top tips, updates and other useful information, but at the end of the day social media is SOCIAL, and we all want to enjoy our experience online.

Having some fun content also gives you a bit of personality and avoids your online profile looking like a machine that is constantly churning out content in a robotic way.

If you cannot decide what fun content to post, head over to YouTube and search for funny videos related to what you do. For example, if you're an estate agent or removal company you may search for funny videos related to moving home.

Once you have found a suitable video that sets the right tone for your company, go-ahead and post it. Posts like this are especially popular on a Friday, or at the weekend.

A great example of a brand making great posts like this is Innocence drinks. Their drinks and branding possibly have nothing to do with giraffes at all, but people clearly loved their post below. 99 people retweeted and 35 people Liked what many people might consider to be a post that has nothing to do with what they sell (and yes, they are right... but isn't it a great post?).

Admittedly, Innocence drinks is known for its fun branding and your company may not want to go too far down that road, but the point I'm trying to make here is that when it comes to social media, people love content that is light-hearted or contains a fun element that they can associate with.

I don't recommend posting too many fun posts like this unless it's in line with your brand and your brand message, but it's important to get a good mix of content and fun content should be part of that.

Selfies. Everyone's at it

↩ Reply ⇄ Retweet ★ Favorite ••• More ¶ HootSuite

RETWEETS   FAVORITES
99   35

10:03 AM - 20 Jul 2013   Flag media

Blend fun and current affairs

Everybody loves to know what's going on in the world, and what is trending. For some people this may be football or other sports, for other people it may be local current affairs and celebrity gossip. Providing a post to your audience that includes something newsworthy whilst making it fun or amusing can increase the interactions dramatically.

To make it even more powerful, make sure to use a hashtag where a conversation is taking place.

In September 2014, I made a post on Twitter just before the Scottish referendum was taking place. I used the hashtag #Indyref which was by far and away the number 1 hashtag being used for discussion on Twitter on this topic.

The post also included a link to a funny article saying that Nessie (the Loch Ness monster) had decided it was a NO vote in the referendum and sightings had been made of Nessie who had migrated south to England.

The article was very funny and by combining this with the right hashtag, my post got a large number of retweets. The total reach of this post exceeded more than 50,000 people on Twitter. This is a great example of how to make your Twitter profile go viral with good content.

Here is the link to the post:
https://Twitter.com/Advance2Britain/status/51223347156 6430208

18. Post top tips

Providing a top tip or other similar content that adds value to your followers can really make a difference. It helps when using the ATM model mentioned earlier and it demonstrates your expertise.

Top tips should be relevant to what you offer and your target audience.

Here are some examples:

The Bookkeeper

If you are a bookkeeper, post top tips on how to do effective bookkeeping such as using a highlighter pen to track data entry or visiting the HMRC (in the UK) or IRS (in the USA) website regularly for updates. You may also want to include key dates for submitting financial documents.

Now what sort of a business would not want to follow a bookkeeper that gives great advice like this? Heck, I'm always afraid of missing important deadlines and updates from HMRC so following this account would really add value.

If I need a bookkeeper, one glance at their profile on social media and I can clearly see they know what they're talking about. Now might be a great time for me to get in contact to see if they can help me out. A few top tips, and a sale is completed!

The Florist

A florist that gives great tips on how to look after beautiful bouquets of flowers and that makes suggestions for which flowers are best to have, depending on the season, will gain a lot of respect with followers online. Top tips might include the right food to give flowers, the right colours for the right room in the house, or even how often to change the water in the vase.

Imagine I have been following this florist for several months and Valentine's Day is fast approaching. I log on to Facebook and I see a beautiful bouquet of 12 red roses in my newsfeed with tips on what makes a perfect gift that goes well with them. I'm online anyway and have been thinking about what to get for the special day.

This florist I have been following clearly is passionate about their products and knows what they are talking about. That simple post which has been posted at just the right time will definitely entice me to place an order.

19. Post local content

Everybody loves buying locally and supporting local businesses as well as supporting local events.

You can easily gain attention and start conversations by talking about what is happening locally. If there are major events taking place, then share them on your newsfeed. Sharing posts from local companies will also help.

You can also use local hashtags such as the country, state, city or village you are based in.

Tip: On Twitter, why not use Twitter Lists to create a list of profiles so that you can quickly see what they are talking about. Doing this means that you don't need to follow them, and you can filter out other posts that normally appear in your newsfeed.

For every day of the year there is always a national or worldwide event and it's well worth promoting these and getting involved in conversations around events that are relevant to your business and your target audience.

To find out about different days of the year, visit this site: https://www.daysoftheyear.com/

If you provide yummy cakes, then get involved in national baking week - and use #NBW in your posts (remember to include an image of a yummy cake and possibly post it when people are not only online, but also hungry!).

If you are offering something slightly healthier than yummy cakes, then you may want to get involved in national vitamin D awareness week – or #NVDAW for short.

Businesses that sell to other businesses can take advantage of Organise your desk day, Salesperson day, Leave the office earlier day, Improve your office day and much more, while food-related businesses can take advantage of Egg day, Noodle day, Dessert day and so on...

These are just examples and there are lots more days and weeks to celebrate each year including themed weeks and months such as Random Acts of Kindness Week. People love to know about events, especially if they are about making a difference in the world.

FREE Days of the Year list!

I have created a spreadsheet list of over 1,000 Days & Months of the Year, including a link to the webpage for each one.

I normally sell this separately, but you can access it for free using the link below.

https://social.darrenhignett.com/daysoftheyear

Once you have accessed the spreadsheet, make sure to save a copy by clicking on File >> Make a Copy.

Please note that the dates change for many of the events so the first column includes the usual month that each event takes place rather than a specific date.

I have included a column at the end with a more accurate date for many of the events, but I can't guarantee that these are precise.

I recommend clicking on the URLs in the document to find out the exact date for this year or next year.

21. Create Fun-motional posts

Besides being a made-up word, fun-motional posts are social media posts that are fun and engaging while cleverly promoting your products or services.

I started creating these types of posts many years ago and they have proven to be highly successful for me and my many clients.

A fun-motional post typically starts with a funny picture or image, followed by wording that ends with a theme such as "If you are struggling with this, we can also help".

Let's take an example...

I once posted a picture of what looked like an old man. In the picture was fictional quoted wording from him that said, "Managing my marketing is not stressful ~ John, aged 21 years".

The suggestion here is that he has become stressed and aged managing his marketing. All I needed to do was add wording to my post that adds context and include a clever call to action along the lines of "If you find marketing stressful or time consuming, make sure to get help. Get in touch to find out how we can support you...".

Chapter 5: Content Creation

In this chapter, I focus on ways to come up with content as well as how to optimise your content to get better results.

Coming up with content

22. Use your competitor's profiles as a source for ideas (and content)

Stuck for ideas on content?

Visit your competitor's profiles and write down some ideas. It's amazing how a quick glance at what other people are doing can help to inspire you with new ideas... and often ideas on how to do things better than your competitors!

23. Use a content finder tool and consider RSS feeds

There are various tools that you can use to find content for posting on social media.

In this section, we are focusing more on content such as articles, rather than video content. In other words, the ideas in this section are more for LinkedIn and Twitter rather than Instagram or TikTok.

RSS feeds are a great place to start and if you aren't sure what they are, it's a way of being able to pull updates from a website such as a new or blog post feed.

If you have an RSS feed for your blog post, then someone can use it to get updates when you add new blogs.

Wikipedia describes RSS feeds as:

"RSS is a web feed that allows users and applications to access updates to websites in a standardized, computer-readable format. These feeds can, for example, allow a user to keep track of many different websites in a single news aggregator".

FeedSpot and Feedly are great examples of tools which helps you to find content from RSS feeds.

Sometimes the content isn't exactly what you want, and you will need to scan through the posts and the links to see how good they are, but they can save you a lot of time researching topics and coming up with content ideas.

I use Feedspot regularly and Feedly is a good solution. You can also find other alternatives by searching for "best RSS readers" on Google.

This article also has some good options:

https://zapier.com/blog/best-rss-feed-reader-apps

Google Alerts is also a great solution. Head over to Google Search, type in a keyword then when you get the results, click on 'News'. You will then see all the latest updates on that keyword.

At the bottom of the page, Google offers to keep you up to date on this keyword by subscribing to Google Alerts.

Once subscribed you will receive regular emails with updates on that keyword. The frequency of the updates can be set and managed very easily.

An insurance business wanting to post content about updates to the industry and regulations might set up Alerts for keywords such as 'home insurance', 'auto insurance' or 'life insurance'. Once they receive the updates in their inbox, they can easily copy and paste the links into social media or through a third-party app.

Optimising Content

24. Blog, email, and social media all working together

Under the chapter "The Integrated Approach", I go through ways to integrate different marketing channels and activities. Blog, email and social media are, however, worth mentioning here in the content chapter as the 3 of them work together very well when it comes to effective content marketing.

Once you have written a blog, you need to promote it and push out the content to your audience, so they are aware of it. The best way to do this is by using multiple channels.

Some people really embrace social media, using it and checking their newsfeed several times throughout the day whilst other people prefer to use other channels, only checking their Facebook or LinkedIn profiles on a weekly or less frequent basis.

By combining email, blogs and social media together you can provide the right content in various forms to the right audience through the channels they prefer.

In other words, if you write a great blog, you can post it on social media and drive customers to it as well as include it in your email marketing.

Similarly, you can use email to drive readers to your blog posts. You can also include links in your emails to content on social.

On your blog page, you can also offer readers the chance to subscribe so that they will receive an email update when you post a new blog.

Finally, remember to include the ability for readers of your blog to share your fantastic content on social media with the right share buttons.

There's no point posting content when nobody is online and, while there's always a chance that somebody may see your posts later on, the chances are your post could be a lot more effective by posting at a different time.

If you want your content to be truly effective, then you need to post interesting content when your target audience is most likely to see it, and there are various scheduling tools that can help you identify when the best time is to post.

For Facebook, you can also use Facebook Insights to understand when people are online to help you determine the best days and times to post.

Finding the right times and days to post may not be a perfect science as a fan who has been online in the evenings for the last month may not necessarily be online in the evenings in the future, but the good news is that using tools to identify the best time to post give a great indication for when there is a higher chance of engaging with your audience.

Once you have worked out the best time to post, use this time to post out content in the future, and then track to see how many more people saw your posts and interacted with them.

Finding out the best time to post content should take less than 20 minutes to do and will improve the visibility of your future posts.

I've seen many articles and studies that identify the best times to post on social media and, unfortunately, the best times depend on your target audience and what platforms you use.

If you don't want to spend too much time understanding this in detail then Tuesday, Wednesday, and Thursday at 10 am local time are the most effective times.

Other time slots should include when people are taking breaks such as at lunch time, early in the morning before starting work and in the evenings.

26. Distribute your content TO your audience

Sometimes you may find that despite your many efforts to generate fantastic content to your followers on your timeline, your audience is listening but not necessarily interacting.

By sharing your content on other forums such as social media groups, then you will be distributing content to your audience that are not currently listening in a more direct way.

Think of it like this: posting on your own social media feed will mostly be seen by your followers, fans or connections.

Posting in a LinkedIn or Facebook group will be seen by people in your target audience who aren't currently following.

A solar-power installer might post in a Facebook group that's set up to provide sustainability and energy saving tips.

This group is also their target audience as they are interested in sustainability and saving energy... two features or benefits of what they offer!

By doing this, you will not only raise awareness of your brand, but you will also encourage more interactions and grow your fan or follower base as a result.

Try to find a new community or Facebook or LinkedIn group every week and write a post that adds value.

Chapter 6: Smart Content Tactics

In this chapter, we will be covering from smart ways to get be more effective and get better results out of your social media posts.

27. Set up a Social Media calendar

Setting up a social media calendar 6 to 12 months in advance can help generate ideas and plan in advance. It may take a bit of time initially to set this up but as you come across certain events such as relevant exhibitions, charity events or other activities of the year then you can add them to your social media calendar to make sure that you post out the right content on the right day.

There is nothing worse than discovering a major event you could participate in on social media a few days after it has occurred. Set up a social media calendar today and add to it throughout the year.

FREE Scheduling Calendar!

I have created a 12-month social media calendar full of quotes, questions and other things that you can post.

I normally sell this separately, but you can access this highly valuable template for free using the link below.

https://social.darrenhignett.com/socialmediacalendar

Once you have accessed the calendar, make sure to save a copy by clicking on File >> Make a Copy.

There are separate tabs for each month. Please note that I update this template over time so you might find that some of the months aren't in sync.

For example, if you have bought this book toward the end of the calendar year then it might not have the last few months of the year as I have updated November, December etc so that the template has 12 full months for the upcoming year.

The good news is that you have access to all future updates so you can check back at any time to access an updated template!

28. Ask people to share your post

When creating a post, don't be afraid to ask people to share your content. There is always an argument and trade-off here that if you keep asking people to share your posts you may come across as being desperate.

You may even be considered cheeky, but the hard truth is that posts which ask people to share, get a higher rate of sharing than those that don't. Let me put that another way: do not ask people to share, and they won't. Ask people to share and they might.

Please note that I strongly urge you not to ask people to share every post that goes out and make sure that what you are posting out is of value to your audience.

It doesn't have to be a top tip. It could be funny, or it could include some amazing fact that your followers would like to share with their friends.

Did you know on Twitter more posts are retweeted when you use the word retweet rather than the abbreviation RT?

Only use the word RT when you are struggling to fit what you want to say into your post.

29. Tease people with click through

What do I mean by this? Simply put, we live in a world where we all have busy lives, information overload and short attention spans and because of this, people interact more with shorter posts.

If, for example, you want to tell people the top five best ways to do something, then rather than listing them all in a tedious, long Facebook post or doing five separate posts on Facebook, you can give them this advice in a blog and post out to your followers to let them know the blog exists. Don't just say "here is a blog" … as most people will just look at the post, not click on the link and decide to read it later (when in reality their busy lives will mean they won't).

Instead, tease them with a post that makes them want to click on the link and read the article.

When writing your post in a teasing way, make sure to use words that get them wanting more. Below are some examples, showing better ways to put together a post.

Original Post:
I have just written an article about how video is important for your business. Here's the link with more information

Whilst there is nothing strictly wrong with this post, you have already told the readers that video is important, and not really given them anything exciting to think about.

Yes, maybe they do want to understand how video is important to the business so they will click on the link, but below are some alternatives worth considering:

Here are six ways video can help your business grow...
Want to grow your business? Here is how video can help...

These posts create intrigue and make you want to read on to find out exactly how using video can help you grow your business. It is difficult sometimes to convey a message or explain what you are trying to say on social media in such a small post (especially on Twitter where there is a limit of 280 characters).

When the message is complex or long, then the aim of social media should be to get people's attention and direct them to your website or blog for more information where you can explain the benefits in more detail.

When sharing content, you can make it more effective by bringing targeted people into the conversation.

For example, if you find a great piece of content from somebody and you want to share it, make sure to mention them in the post. It not only gets their attention, but they may decide to share the content as well with their connections or follower.

Another example is if you are attending an event and you know certain people who will be there. You may want to share the details of the event and mention that you are looking forward to meeting great people such as ABC or DEF - and then include them in the same post.

On most platforms including Instagram, LinkedIn and Twitter, you can add people by starting with the @ symbol. If for example, you want to mention someone by the name of John Blogs on LinkedIn then type @ followed by his first name. As you type the first few letters, all contacts whose name starts with j, or jo will start to appear in a list.

For Facebook, there are restrictions on who you can mention on your Facebook pages and the person you are trying to mention might have their privacy settings set up to not allow you to mention them.

31. Bulk load 'foundation' content

In an ideal world, we would have time to sit there all day long posting content and interacting with people, but unfortunately if you're anything like me I'm guessing you have a lot of work to do!

The best way to be effective when building content is to create a schedule of, what I refer to as, foundation content. This is content which is non-time sensitive yet still adds value to your followers.

If you build foundation content for at least a month in advance that goes out daily (so that's a minimum of 30 posts on Facebook for example) then you will have saved up enough time for posting content on current affairs or interacting with people throughout the week or month.

Another great advantage of doing this is that you can post out content at times when followers are online, but you are in meetings, travelling or even taking time out on a break! (Also consider the fact that people also interact on social media at the weekends when you may prefer to be with friends and family).

32. Outsource content creation

Content creation can take up a lot of time, and let's not forget that your time is money! There are expert copywriters and social media marketers that can come up with content that gets the attention of your target audience.

You may even find that having a second perspective means your content is less technical than if you write it yourself.

If you don't want to outsource the whole process of writing and scheduling content, then you can still save a considerable amount of time by using websites such as Fiverr or PeoplePerHour to research and write content ideas for you.

This saves time researching and brainstorming. All you need to do is make edits to what they have written or write posts based off the ideas they have given. If you're not aware of Fiverr, it's a website where people provide marketing and other services from as little as $5... it's well worth considering. Especially if you are lacking inspiration (and time) for good content.

Here are the links for websites where you can outsource to someone online:

www.fiverrr.com
www.peopleperhour.com
www.elance.com

For more information on why outsourcing can make a huge difference to your business read this blog 'Don't waste previous time, outsource':

https://darrenhignett.blogspot.com/2015/05/dont-waste-precious-time-outsource.html

Meme's have become very popular in the last few years and they are a great way to add some light-heartedness to your posts.

Over the last few years, I have successfully used memes as a clever way to promote my customers' products.

Images such as Robert Downey Jr. rolling his eyes along with the words 'And he said he would do his finances by himself' or a puzzled child with the words 'and you're telling me I can save hours if someone else does my paperwork' are great ways to grab the attention of the target audience of a bookkeeper or admin support business.

Worded properly, it also sends a subtle message of what the benefits are of the services that they provide.

You can use Canva or Stencil to create your own meme, but there are also various online apps that are free that you can use that are dedicated to creating memes with your own wording.

I use Make A Meme (https://makeameme.org/).

34. Use custom overlay links for greater sales enquiry generation

Ideally every time you do a social media post, you should include a link to your own website and blogs, but this just isn't possible.

If you are posting once or twice a day for example on social media, then potentially you would need to write up to two blogs or articles a day – or find a good reason to include a link to your website.

Of course, not every post you make needs to point to an external article but the point I am trying to make here is that it simply isn't possible to be the only person providing relevant articles to your followers. That is where apps such as Snip.ly come in (https://sniply.io/).

If you find a third-party website providing some great top tips relevant to your followers, you can post the article on social media to your followers, linking to the content of the external website - and you can still be in control of the lead capture process!

How does that work? I hear you ask. Well, what Snip.ly does is it allows you to cleverly place a call to action (complete with link or button) on that third-party website.

The website and article can still be viewed as normal, but your custom message is overlaid on the page.

When your follower clicks on the link in your post and visits that website, they can read the article and then click on your call to action to either visit your website or contact you.

Here's an example:

An accountant might find an interesting article on how to manage finances that is posted by an accountancy software firm such as Intuit or SAGE.

He or she can post this great article to their followers (since it is highly relevant to them and shows the accountant is sharing useful information) and when the follower reads the article, they will see a banner at the bottom of the screen that says "Get your finances in order with a free business review" - along with the social media bio image for the accountancy firm and a link through to their contact us page on their website.

In other words, the accountant posts an article on someone else's website. Followers who click on the link can read the article but still be presented with a call to action, re-directing them back to the accountant to get in touch.

There are various alternatives to snip.ly, including JotURL and exitbar.io.

Creating visual posts

Before we move on to different tactics for different social media platforms, I would like to share some tips for creating visual images on social media.

Creating visual posts can be very time-consuming and require a certain level of knowledge on how to create them. Added to this, there are also issues over what images you can use and are copyrighted.

There are some great websites where you can purchase images but if you are doing this regularly then the costs can quickly add up.

Having said that, visual posts will always get more attention and interactions than text-based posts and will also look a lot more professional. One option is to take pictures yourself, and don't be afraid to do this.

As well as purchasing images, there are also a number of websites with royalty free images and tools to allow you to create your own visual posts for free or relatively low cost.

I have listed some examples of these sites below:

Royalty Free Images

Note: This list is not exhaustive, and you may find other sites with better images for your line of business. Make sure to check the terms of usage on each website as some sites offer royalty free as well as copyrighted images. I am not responsible for any downloads you make that may breach copyright!

https://unsplash.com/
www.freeimages.com/
http://commons.wikimedia.org/wiki/Main_Page
www.pixabay.com
www.pexels.com

You can also use Google images to search for images that are labelled for re-use.

Tools for creating visual posts

There are several applications available, but the following 2 tools are my preferred tools for creating visual posts. I use them on a regular basis, and they really make a difference to the quality of posts on social media –for very little time, cost and effort.

Canva
www.Canva.com
This tool has pre-defined images sizes so that you can take an existing image and resize it for posting on Twitter, Facebook, Pinterest etc. It also includes size formats for email marketing, blogging and a range of other uses.

Canva also includes a range of free images as well as images that cost a mere $1 to buy. You can also upload your own images and add text and background colours.

Canva saves your work so that you can download and re-use them again in the future.

Stencil
https://getstencil.com/app
This tool has a library of images (on the subscription version only) that you can use, and you can also upload your own images. You can then overlay wording on to the image for higher impact. This is particularly useful with blogs as you can have the title of the blog or some other call to action appear on the image when it is posted on social media.

Stencil also allows you to add effects to the image such as making it blurred, darkened, added clarity or even an orange peel effect.

Similar to Canva, the images can also be saved, and you can select the format size whether it is for a Facebook post, LinkedIn post or even for using in an Ad.

There is a free version but for a few dollars a month, it is well worth getting the Pro version if you intend to do a lot of visual posts on social media.

If you are still not convinced about visual posts, put half an hour aside to create three or four posts. Then schedule them out at a rate of one per week.

It's not a lot, but it's a great start and will make a huge difference to your newsfeed appearance - for just half an hour's work.

We will now focus on tactics that are specific to individual social media platforms. Over the next few chapters we will go through ways to boost your business using features that are specific to Instagram, Twitter, Facebook and so on.

You might find that some features on one platform also exist on another so there is some duplication – especially as social media platforms seem to copy each other to avoid losing out!

I've grouped them in the way I think is best and some features work better on some platforms than others. Hashtags on Facebook, for example, a almost useless while on Instagram and Twitter, they can be a lot more effective.

Chapter 7: Instagram

35. Include 30 hashtags on Instagram posts

Instagram allows you to include up to 30 hashtags with each post and, unlike Twitter, it's a lot more acceptable to include as many hashtags as possible in your post.

So, how many hashtags should you use?

To get the best exposure with your content, use as many hashtags as you can. There might be times when you can't find enough relevant hashtags, or you are in a rush to get content out. In these circumstances you might post less than 30 but it will impact how many people see your posts.

With Instagram, you are allowed to follow hashtags as well as other profiles. If I follow the hashtag #inspirationalquotes and you post an inspirational quote using this hashtag, then it's possible that your post will appear in my newsfeed — even if I'm not following you!

Note: It's recommended to vary your hashtags and keep them as relevant as possible to the post. As well as following a hashtag, it's also possible to 'untag' you by selecting 'don't show for this hashtag'.

Top Tip: You can find relevant hashtags by typing into the search box in Instagram. If, for example, you are looking for hashtags related to healthy eating then as you start to type a phrase such as '#health' then suggested hashtags, along with how popular they are, will be shown.

Top Tip: You can also make your post clutter free and easy to read by hiding your hashtags. To do this, simply put them in a comment on your post rather than the main post wording. All you have to do is post your content without the hashtags, then comment on your own post with the hashtags!

36. Create a bio page for your Instagram bio link

This sounds complicated but it isn't.

Instagram is a great platform for engaging with your target audience and although it depends on your business, Instagram typically achieves more likes, follows and reach than other mainstream social media platforms. It does, however, have one major drawback - it's harder to organically drive people to your website.

Anyone using Instagram for business will be aware that you cannot include clickable links in standard posts to your feed and links are only possible in Stories if you have over 10,000 followers (which everyone has, right?).

The only clickable link for most Instagram businesses is the one that appears in their bio.

If you are a regular blogger or a business trying to promote a special offer - and want to use Instagram to increase visitors to your website, then it can be a challenge.

The simplest and cheapest but the least effective of the four ways to drive Instagrammers to your website is to include a link in your post and ask them to copy and paste it into their browser.

Many people won't have the desire (or knowhow) to copy the link and open the browser to paste in the link. On a desktop is easier but since Instagram is seen by almost everyone on a mobile phone then this makes the task even harder.

Only people who are super keen to visit the link will spend the time copying and pasting the link.

There is, however, a better solution... At Think Twice Marketing, we use Shorby. An app that allows you to have a selection of links available when someone clicks on your bio link.

Although the bio can only have one clickable link, multiple links tools like this allow you to create a mini pop-up menu on your phone with multiple links. These links can be easily edited or removed and can include links to specific blogs, your home or contact page or even to WhatsApp or Email so that they can contact you directly.

Using a multiple links tool allows your audience to quickly find the page you want them to visit on your website directly from your Instagram bio. All you need to do in posts is tell people to click on the link in your bio.

You can see how we use a multiple links tool by visiting Think Twice Marketing on Instagram and clicking on our bio link.

As well as Shorby, consider Linktree, Lnk.Bio and Linkin.bio by Later. If you use Instagram a lot, then also consider using Later for posting content.

37. Use location in your posts on Instagram

People love supporting local and often want to engage with local people on social media. When you post on Instagram, make sure to spend a few extra seconds to add your location.

I also suggest varying your location slightly for different posts. If you live in a suburb of a city such as London or New York, then you can post from that city or using the name of the suburb.

Doing this increases the chances of you being found as different people will search for people using different locations in their search.

Chapter 8: Twitter

38. Pin a great post to the top of your newsfeed

Facebook and Twitter allow you to pin one of your posts to the top of your newsfeed. There are two ways you can approach this and the first one is to use a post that shows what you do and the benefits to a potential new follower who visits your profile.

The second approach is to post a hugely popular post you have done which has a lot of Likes or Comments.

Alternatively, if you are running a promotion for a short period of time then you may want to pin the promotional post to the top of your newsfeed so that people can find it easily. Either way, make sure that you pin something that makes people want to take an interest in and follow you.

Unfortunately, LinkedIn and Instagram do not allow you to pin posts to the top which is a shame — especially for LinkedIn as I'm sure many companies would like to pin updates to the top of their company page.

39. Join hashtag hours on Twitter

These are especially popular among small businesses, and you could easily spend your entire week joining various hashtag hours on Twitter.

So, what is a hashtag hour? It is an hour (obviously!) where you can talk to other people and promote your business on Twitter using a specific hashtag. If you're in Dorset, UK for example then you may join #Dorsethour which currently runs every Tuesday from 19:30 to 20:30.

To join in, simply login to Twitter, go to the search box and type #Dorsethour (or whatever the relevant hour is you are joining). You will then be presented with the many posts and conversations that are taking place.

From here you can reply to or retweet a post. You can also write your own post but remember to include the relevant hashtag when you tweet so that other people who are joining in can interact with your post.

Hashtag hours are a great way to build relationships with other businesses and get yourself found on Twitter but be careful as it can take up a lot of your time.

If you are limited for time but want to join these conversations regularly then my recommendation would be to join at the beginning of an hour for 5 to 10 minutes, then go away and do other things before returning to the conversation later on (I tend to find the last 15 minutes is best).

Doing it this way you will only spend around 20 minutes or so rather than a full 60 minutes which can be very time-consuming when you are joining several #hours in a week. Either way, since most hashtag hours are in the evenings, it is still time used up late in the day.

Note: it is important to join in conversations and interact rather than just blasting out a few posts with the relevant hashtag. The purpose of #hours are to build relationships, not to promote your services in a one-way communication.

40. Upload contacts to Twitter

Did you know that you can upload your contacts into Twitter and then follow them? Twitter allows you to connect to your email platform (such as Gmail) and it will search for your contacts on Twitter.

Once it has found matches, it will then ask you if you would like to follow them all by clicking on the 'Follow All' button. You can also follow them manually at this stage or deselect ones that you don't want to follow.

This feature does not always find a huge amount of your contacts as it depends on your contacts settings in Twitter. They must have the option enabled that allows them to be discovered by searching for their email address.

If you have been in contact with people via email, this feature is great as it increases the interactions with them and helps to build trust.

Here's instructions on how to import your contacts on Twitter:

https://help.twitter.com/en/using-twitter/upload-your-contacts-to-search-for-friends

By creating a public Twitter list around a particular theme or topic, people can subscribe to that list to get regular updates. You can also gain credibility with the people that you add to the list.

If you are a specialist in providing updates on what's happening locally then you may add local attractions and restaurants to a public Twitter list called "what's going on in [town/county]".

When you add people to the list, they will be notified. They may even promote the list themselves as it is useful for their followers. Now that you have the list set up with some good members added, people can visit the list and get some great updates.

I have more great ideas for how you can use Twitter Lists in my blog "7 Ways to Use Twitter Lists Effectively". Here is the link:

https://darrenhignett.blogspot.com/2015/05/7-ways-to-use-twitter-lists-effectively.html

This action also applies to Pinterest, TikTok and Instagram (and to some extent, LinkedIn).

If you follow potential customers, most social media platforms will send them an email to let them know you are following them. Right there you have just been given free email marketing.

Providing your bio is set up correctly and your profile is of interest to them then there is a chance they will follow you back.

The result being that they can then regularly see your newsfeed of great content (which you have put together after reading the previous chapters of this book!).

It's important to consider that people don't know you exist on social media until you get their attention, and following potential customers is a great way to say, "I am here!"

If you are worried that this can take a lot of time, it needn't. If you just follow 50 profiles per week on Instagram or Twitter, then this is 2600 profiles you have followed over the year.

Even a 1% return rate converting customers means you have found 26 customers from an activity that should take less than five minutes to do every week. You can also apply this to LinkedIn by inviting around 5-10 people to connect with you every day.

Note: we are not talking about aggressive following and unfollowing. Platforms such as Twitter and Instagram have measures in place to stop this and you will risk having your account locked.

Top Tip: Put aside 10 minutes every day with a target to follow 10 profiles on Instagram or Twitter that are relevant and invite 2 or 3 people on LinkedIn to connect. You can increase your targets if you want to, but this activity shouldn't take up a lot of your time.

43. Send a direct message to new followers on Twitter

This method is controversial due to the number of low value automated direct messages (or DMs) that people receive. There are many people out there on Twitter automatically sending direct messages to people who follow them, and it can be quite annoying.

The main reason it's annoying is that 99% of these posts don't add any value to the new follower. This results in a high unfollow rate. Having said that, a well worded direct message to anyone who follows you will create leads and can yield a good return on investment.

When using this option, it's highly dependent upon the wording really adding value and on the quality of the people that follow you.

A free e-book, discount code or something similar should be used. Do not – and I repeat absolutely do not – thank people for following on Twitter and then ask them to Like you on Facebook.

Now that you have them on Twitter, don't try to drive them away to a different social media platform that they actually might not use.

This kind of message adds no value to new followers whatsoever. If the message doesn't add value to the new follower, then don't send it out.

44. Monitor keywords and set up a filter on Twitter

Filters allow you to find people or conversations that relate to your products and services. If for example you specialise in products for weddings, then you can easily go on to social media and search for specific terms such as 'on their engagement'. This will return people who are congratulating friends that have just got engaged.

You have now found potential customers and what you do next is up to you! You could add them to a list, follow them, or join in the conversation and congratulate them (although that may freak them out as they don't know who you are). A better solution might be to reply by offering them a link to a blog on how to prepare for the big day.

A further example is a company that offers opportunities for people wanting to work from home. In this scenario you can easily search for specific terms such as 'need a job' or 'made redundant'.

With this example you would need to be very careful how you approach what you do next. Whatever you decide to do the important point is that by searching the correct keywords, you can instantly see who potential customers are.

You may need to play around with finding the right keywords and don't be surprised if the content you get back in the early stages is a bit strange but keep testing different keywords to see what results you get.

45. Host a conversation

We have talked about joining conversations (or hashtag hours) on Twitter but why not host your own?

This takes up a lot more time but allows you to gain a lot of credibility with your audience and stand out from your competition. It also means you have a varied and different type of content that is highly engaging.

Hosting a conversation could include an hour when customers can ask you questions, or it could be around a particular industry topic where leaders in the industry join in.

You may also want to vary the topic every week or month to keep fans engaged.

Twitter offers a feature where you can host a live broadcast that's audio only. There has been a huge growth in recent years in people listening to audio content such as podcasts and audiobooks -and Twitter Spaces is Twitter's attempt to be part of this growth.

Twitter Spaces can be scheduled in advance, recorded and can have up to 15 speakers at the same time.

Imagine a garden retail outlet that offers plants, ornaments, and other stuff such as gardening equipment. They might want to run a Twitter Space weekly with top tips for a great looking garden.

One session might include advice for plant care, along with recommendations for what plant food to use.

It might also include tips for trimming hedges and bushes – along with suggestions for what gardening equipment is best for a neatly looking hedgerow.

There are all sorts of ways that you can use Twitter Spaces to engage your target audience.

Using Twitter ads, you can easily set up a post that talks about the product you offer or the benefits of your services. The post will then appear as sponsored in other people's newsfeed.

Make sure to target your ads so that only your target audience see your ad. If you only serve a local community or area, then you don't want to pay every time someone who is thousands of miles away clicks on your ad.

48. Use GIFs on Twitter

Visual content is highly effective but creating videos can take time and can be costly. Enter... GIFs.

Animation can make a social media post stand out and Twitter allows you to quickly add a GIF image to your post.

Doing this not only saves you time creating images or videos, but they are also a great way to stand out and increase engagement.

GIFs are also a great way to stand out in emails and on your website, if used properly.

Chapter 9: LinkedIn

49. Get your LinkedIn endorsements and recommendations up to scratch

If you use LinkedIn, then this is important. Many customers make their decision before buying a product on how good or bad its reviews are.

In 2013, Zendesk did a survey that found as many as 90% of respondents claimed that online reviews influenced their buying decisions. Today, reviews have become more important than ever before.

LinkedIn doesn't do reviews, but having recommendations and endorsements are the same, on a personal level. Potential customers may visit your LinkedIn profile to see if you are the type of person or business they can trust to work with.

Having a recommendation will reduce this barrier to purchasing and help to favour you over your competition.

Make sure your endorsements reflect your current skill sets relevant to the services you offer. If you were previously an accountant but decided to take a career change into marketing (and yes - possibly a strange example!) then make sure your endorsements are for marketing activities such as social media or advertising and not for payroll management or handling tax returns.

I wouldn't buy marketing support from someone who has more endorsements for tax saving than online marketing and I wouldn't hire an accountant who is better known for their content writing than financial management! Would you?

50. Use a connection to reach someone

When you get approached by someone directly, asking if you are interested in what they do then there tends to a resistance.

At the back of the mind, we wonder who this person or brand is, and should we trust them, but we are more likely to take an interest if that person has been recommended. Afterall, they must be trustworthy if a friend or colleague we know, and trust recommends them.

If you want to approach a potential client on LinkedIn and you discover that you both share a connection, then you can always ask your contact how well they know them and if they would be ok to recommend or at least, introduce you to them.

Introducing rather than recommending might not sound as powerful but the mere act of sending an email that says 'I would like to introduce you to a contact (or friend) of mind who offers a service you might be interested in' – will actually be interpreted subconsciously by the recipient as a form of recommendation.

If you are worried that your contact won't introduce you or will feel annoyed at being asked to do it, don't worry too much. Research also shows that people love to help with simple or easy requests like this.

They usually feel like they are making a difference and will be pleased to be seen as being the one person who can help. Just remember to thank them.

It's still possible that someone might not want to help. In which case, don't be too pushy in your approach. A simple message saying 'I was wondering – and would be really grateful – if you could help me out' is enough. There's no need to keep chasing.

51. Use Google search to find LinkedIn contacts

Finding the right contacts within the right companies can sometimes be difficult and searching on LinkedIn doesn't always show the results you want as it hides parts of a contacts name (partly because LinkedIn wants you to pay for their premium edition to improve the way you reach your target contacts) – but here is a great way to find your LinkedIn contacts…. on Google:

Visit Google and type in the keywords of the person you are trying to reach. If you are targeting the Operations Director, then your search will look like this:

Site: LinkedIn.com "Operations Director"

Or…

LinkedIn Operations Director

This will return profile links of people on LinkedIn who have the word "Operations Director" in their profile.

You may want to narrow this down further by adding extra search terms such as "Present (6 months)" to only find the contacts who have been in their current role for 6 months.

You can also add other data such as location. For example, if you are looking for sales directors in Birmingham then type in the following:

Sales Director Birmingham LinkedIn

Once you have found the right contacts, you can try to establish contact with them on LinkedIn or in other marketing campaigns.

52. Use a LinkedIn Messaging campaign

LinkedIn allows you to create adverts that work in the same way as on Facebook, Twitter and other platforms with objectives to drive people to a website or to engage with your content, for example.

LinkedIn also lets you set up a campaign that allows you to directly message LinkedIn contact. Messaging is proven to get better results than an advert appearing in a newsfeed, and it's seen as being more personal on LinkedIn.

Using a LinkedIn messaging ad, you can target the right person, in the right role and at the right company with a special offer.

Using LinkedIn ads, you can quickly target people based on their professional profile. Examples include being able to display your sales software and sales training ad only to sales directors of telecommunications companies in the London or Manchester area, your ad for laboratory equipment only visible to purchasing managers in laboratory-based companies or your recruitment services to appear as an ad to hiring and HR managers in companies with more than 500 employees.

These are of course, only examples, but you get the idea how you can target the right person in the right type of organisation as well as target based on the location and size of the business.

53. Build your connections and personalise your message on LinkedIn

LinkedIn shows other people the total number of connections you have but if you have over 500 then it simply says "500+".

Reaching this number gives added credibility. If you are a professional networker or industry leader for example but only have 60 connections, what does that say about you? The first thought is that you are not that well connected, especially for a networker!

Try to achieve over 500 connections with people you know (customers, suppliers, work colleagues) and when you invite them to connect remember to personalise the message including their name. It shows you care about them!

Also, stay organised by reviewing your connections and adding categories to them so that you know how many suppliers, customers etc. you are connected to. This helps for future marketing activities.

54. Endorse, thank and congratulate your contacts weekly on LinkedIn

These are all great ways to get the attention of – and earn bonus points from – your contacts. If you want to get in my good books, feel free to visit my profile on LinkedIn and endorse me for book writing or social media!

Ok, enough of the self-promotion – you get the idea. People love being thanked, endorsed or congratulated on their new job, work anniversary or birthday and the great thing about LinkedIn is that it helpfully reminds you about many of these events!

Why not put it in your diary to connect in some way with at least 10 contacts every week. That's less than 10 minutes effort a week to stay in touch with potentially over 500 contacts over the year!

Note: Don't go randomly endorsing people for skills you don't actually know if they are any good at. Try to be true to yourself when endorsing. I personally treat it as spam when people keep endorsing me for skills that they clearly have never seen me demonstrate – even if I am good at what I do! It has a negative impact on their influence, and it can be annoying.

55. Write an article on LinkedIn instead of (or as well as) a blog site

LinkedIn is also great for writing articles as well as general posts. The next time you go to write a blog, consider using Pulse, especially if you are targeting the B2B market. You could even post the same content on your blog and on LinkedIn.

Just one caution: This does have implications from an SEO perspective around authenticity. In other words, Google will see the same content in two locations and that will have an impact on your SEO rankings of your website.

The pros of having your article seen on LinkedIn by potential customers have to be weighed up against the cons of any SEO efforts you might – or might not – be doing for your website to appear in Google Search.

56. Create a Newsletter on LinkedIn

As well as being able to create an article, you can also create a newsletter and invite your contacts to it.

This is a great way to engage with your contacts who already know you – and it's much quicker than trying to build up an email marketing list of your target audience from scratch.

Email marketing is proven to be highly effective (for more information see my book How to Create a Successful Email Marketing Campaign) and LinkedIn is offering their own version of email marketing.

One point to note: if you are serious about email marketing, using this LinkedIn feature isn't the best solution as it has its limitations.

As far as engaging on LinkedIn with your contacts though, it's a great feature to use as part of the ATM model we discussed earlier in this book.

57. Export your LinkedIn connections for other activities

LinkedIn allows you to export your connections so that you can see them in a spreadsheet. This allows you to do various activities. You can, for example, add notes in a spreadsheet if you are running a campaign – ticking them off if you have contacted them in some way such as via phone.

You can also use the exported contacts to check that your CRM is up to date.

Integration like this has many benefits but just be careful to make sure you comply with your local laws and the terms and conditions of the social media platform you are using. GDPR is important legislation that, like all regulations, you must comply with.

Avoid simply exporting your contacts into a newsletter campaign and emailing them en masse. Your contacts need to have signed up for the newsletter first.

58. A quick LinkedIn Company page strategy

Here is a quick – but co-ordinated – strategy to make your LinkedIn company page works effectively:

Set up a company page and make sure your employees are linked to the company page in their bio (and following the company page). Then ask them to Like and Share posts regularly so that their connections can see them.

That's it! A simple strategy that will increase the visibility of your brand.

If you have a sales representative in the company with 500 connections that he or she is prospecting and building up long term relationships with then every time they share a post from your page, their connections are likely to see that post in their newsfeed.

Multiply that by the number of staff you have, the number of connections they have, and you have some great viral marketing going out to your relevant target market!

Chapter 10: Facebook

Facebook has become the leader among social media platforms, but its recent history has been controversial, and the platform is showing signs of long-term decline.

It has become increasing harder for businesses to get any results out of Facebook without spending money on Facebook Ads.

In this chapter, I will cover some smart ways to use Facebook without spending money but, because of the way Facebook operates nowadays, I have also included a number of tactics for using paid ads.

59. Create a Facebook Event

Facebook seems to give priority to Facebook Group posts and any events that are set up. Have you ever noticed how you get notifications on Facebook saying that a friend is interested in or is going to an event near you?

That's because Facebook is promoting events that have been set up on Facebook pages and giving them more exposure. The reason for this might be to compete with Google who are always promoting local businesses on Google search and through Google Maps but whatever the reason, it's worth considering setting up an event.

You might set up a Facebook Event for a number of reasons: Your restaurant is having a themed event on Saturday; you are hosting a networking event locally or you are planning to launch a new product or service. Whatever the reason, make sure you have it set up as a Facebook Event on your business page.

Here are three top tips to consider:

Top Tip: If you use a platform such as Eventbrite to set up events, you can also integrate it with Facebook so that it sets up the event for you!

Top Tip: Once you have set up a Facebook Event, you can promote it using Facebook Ads. When you visit the event on your Facebook Page, just click on Promote Event to get started.

Top Tip: If you are co-hosting the event with someone else, you can grant them access to edit the Facebook Event. This means that your event will also appear on their Facebook page as well! You can also grant admin access of the event to venues that are hosting your event.

60. Boost a post on Facebook

If you create a post that you think is really good content and effectively promotes your brand, then it's worth spending a small amount boosting the post so that more of your target audience can see it.

In previous sections, I have talked about how Facebook gives more visibility to posts in Facebook Groups as well as to any events that are set up on your page.

One big issue with posting on Facebook pages is that the organic reach has declined considerably over the years. In the early days, Facebook let most people who liked your page see your posts. Then, over the years (for various reasons), Facebook started restricting how many people saw your posts, even if they have already Liked your page.

We won't go into the reasons why here, but the good news is that for just $20/£20 you can boost a post that will reach hundreds of people who might have never heard of your brand before!

You can also select or define who that target audience is. If, for example, you provide business coaching to business owners, then you can target business owner, entrepreneurs and CEOs within a 50-mile radius of your offices.

61. Use Facebook Groups (and LinkedIn)

There was a time when LinkedIn Groups were growing in popularity, whether it was for local networking groups or discussion groups around topics on how to do things better.

Over the last few years, the focus seems to have moved toward using Facebook. Local communities, business networking and all sorts of other groups of people have moved to Facebook to set up a Facebook Group where they can share information and ideas.

Whatever the reason for this, Facebook seem to prioritise posts in Facebook Groups over Facebook business pages.

If you want as many people as possible to see your posts then you are likely to get more visibility by posting in a Facebook Group than on your Facebook page.

Make sure to join relevant groups on Facebook (and LinkedIn) and post valuable content regularly. Make sure that the content is relevant to the group and in line with the rules of the specific group.

LinkedIn Groups have not been fully abandoned and many people still use them. I still recommend using them if they are relevant. My only reservation is that if you had to choose between LinkedIn and Facebook, depending on your business, you might find Facebook gets you better results.

62. Set up your own Facebook Group

As well as joining other groups, you can create your own group and invite people to join. This can be used for various reasons.

Firstly, it can be an exclusive group for existing customers to share ideas and thoughts. Inviting customers to this exclusive group can add value to what you offer and help make the services more enticing.

A group can also be a way to build prospects. A health nutritionist could, for example, set up a group for anyone to join so that they can post positive thoughts and ideas for eating healthy. Maybe with recipe ideas?

I have seen a business coach do this and has built up the group to over 1,500 members. She also posts daily inspirational quotes that everyone likes and interacts with.

The benefit of creating a group like this is that people will join if it's something of interest. And if it's of interest to them, then they are a potential customer. It also helps to raise awareness of your brand as more people join the group and talk about it to other people.

I talk about a Facebook Group, but it could also be a LinkedIn Group as well.

63. Run a Facebook Live session

Facebook Live events are a great way to add a friendly face to a brand and to reach out to your target audience. You can also use the session to provide valuable insights and tips that you might find difficult to do in a worded post.

Another great benefit about using Facebook Live is that Facebook is very good at notifying friends and fans that you are live. It's a great way to grab the attention of your audience.

64. Create an offer on Facebook and boost it

Facebook has a great feature that allows you to create an offer rather than a post. When someone clicks on the call-to-action button in the offer, they will be able to take advantage of the offer.

An example of this might be 25% off your next purchase, valid in the next 48 hours at your store.

This kind of offer is most effective when there is a short period of time to get the coupon and use it. The offer should also be boosted so that a wider audience can see your offer in their timeline, and this can be set up and run from as little as £25 or $25.

65. Message Facebook pages

If you find prospective customers or people on Facebook that you want to build a relationship with then you can easily send a message to the administrator of the Facebook page.

A quick but friendly message asking them to Like your page and letting them know of a promotion or free e-book is a great way to get started, but make sure that the message adds value in some way.

You may find that the admin person for the pages you message is not the right contact within the business, in which case a better option is to ask who the right person is and ask to be introduced. This approach could be considered very direct, but it gets results.

Note: the messaging feature can be disabled on Facebook business pages so you may not be able to always message the company you want. It might also be using an automated bot.

An alternative would be to post on their page directly but be very careful of the wording you use and be selective. Spamming Facebook pages isn't recommended.

66. Set up a Messenger bot on Facebook

Facebook Messenger has become a great way to interact with your target audience and to turn prospects into paying clients.

You can, for example, create a Facebook Ads campaign that directs potential customers to Messenger to have a chat with you. And if you don't have time to prospect with all of them individually? You can set up a bot with a scripted sequence.

This might sound a bit impersonal but there are plenty of large businesses now adopting this for anything from sorting out technical questions and issues to prospecting and signing them up.

There are plenty of Messenger bots available that integrate with Facebook, and we aren't going to go through how to use them in detail here but here's a great way you can use a bot...

Messenger bots allow you to send a message to anyone who has messaged you before or has interacted in some way (for example, using an Ads campaign that uses Messenger).

If you have built up your interactions, then you can quickly and easily send out a message to your prospects via messenger to let them know you have a special offer on or that you have launched a new product.

67. Drive people to your online shop using Facebook Ads

The title says it all! If you are in the tourist trade, then you can create a Facebook Ads campaign to target everybody in a particular age group who has an interest in travel (this could be people who have Liked a branded Facebook page such as hotels.com for example).

Create a powerful call to action in your ad such as money off or free extras then run the campaign with click through to your online shop to place an order.

You may need to do testing to see if changing the wording, or the target audience yields better returns, but you now have a model that you can use over the long term.

The beauty of Pay Per Click is exactly that... you only pay when somebody clicks on your ad, and they should only click on the ad if they are interested in your call to action. If your ad is worded badly then you risk having the wrong people clicking on your ad.

A well worded ad will, however, always have people who aren't ready to buy who click on the link. This is because they are inquisitive rather than ready to buy, but the Pay Per Click costs on Facebook are relatively low and using this sort of campaign properly will allow you to reach a huge number of people in a short period of time.

Remember always to do split testing. Try different ad copies with slightly different wording and different images to see what gets the best results. You may also find advertising at a particular time of year or day of the week gets better results.

With Facebook, you can also pay by impressions rather than by clicks. If you pay by impressions then you will pay for your ads when they appear on people's newsfeed, even if they don't click on it. This has some advantages, such as raising awareness of your brand, but I don't recommend it. Always try to set your spending to pay per click, rather than paying based on impressions.

68. Set up a Facebook Ads with Lead Generation as the objective

There are various ways to set up a Facebook Ads campaign, whether you want to drive people to your website, to Facebook Messenger or to the app store to download your app.

Another great way you can use it is to generate leads within Facebook, by setting the objective of your campaign as 'Lead Generation'.

When you set this as your objective, users who click on your advert will be presented with a pop-up form that you will receive with their details.

The great thing about this is that the user (with their consent) can share their contact details with you without having to fill the form in, as Facebook already has this information. It's highly convenient as the user doesn't have to fill the pain of having to fill the form in and doesn't have to leave Facebook to visit your website.

69. Invite post likes to like your page on Facebook

It's possible that people have liked a post that you published on your Facebook page, but they have not liked your page.

If this is the case, then you can invite them to like your page very quickly using an amazingly simple trick.

To do this, visit the post that has been liked and click or tap where it says how many people have liked.

This will then show you who has liked the post. To the right-hand side of their name, it will either show that they have liked your page, or there will be a button that says 'Invite'.

All you need to do, is click on the Invite button and they will receive a notification that your business page (not you personally) has invited them to like the page.

Inviting people to like your page in this way is especially useful when running a Facebook Ads campaign, as the campaign you run will reach a lot of people who see the ad but who haven't taken the time to visit and like your page.

Inviting them to like your page brings your brand to the front of their mind when they get the notification. If they like your page, it will also mean that they should see your posts in their newsfeed (I say 'should' as it depends on how much they continue to interact with your posts. As we know, Facebook does not let everyone who has liked the page to see the posts).

70. Post tips on Facebook (and LinkedIn) Groups

This idea is blending content and prospecting together in a subtle way. If your business is to manage and provide software and support to companies to help them improve customer services, then posting tips that help them improve customer service will attract their attention.

The content could be an article you found online or could write your own blog. A great topic might be 10 ways to improve customer service.

Once you have the content ready to post, simply visit a LinkedIn or Facebook group where your target market hangs out (a restaurants and hotels group full of hotel managers who have budget and the decision-making authority when it comes to improving the customer service at their venue for example) and write a nice friendly post just to let everybody know that you have written a wonderful blog to help them in their line of business.

You have now helped out your target audience with useful information which will also help convince them as to why they need your services!

If you are writing your own article, then you should also make sure it has a strong call to action at the end. Make sure the call to action is in the article and NOT in the social media group post, otherwise you will scare people off by being too promotional, too early.

The idea of the post on LinkedIn or Facebook is to get the attention of a prospective customer and direct them to your blog or article which adds value to them.

After reading the article you should have provided enough value add and ideas to them along with creating a desire or interest in what you offer.

Chapter 11: Pinterest

71. SEO your Pinterest boards

First of all, a caveat: I'm not covering SEO in this book and have no intention of going into detail about how you can get yourself to page 1 on a Google search.

SEO (or search engine optimisation) is about making your website optimised so that it can be found on page 1 of Google when a customer types in certain keywords related to your product. What I am talking about here, is a clever way to make your Pinterest account appear higher in the Google rankings.

So how do I do this?

Well, at the time of writing this book Google, appears to be indexing Pinterest accounts based on the name of the boards so for example, if you offer widgets in Southampton and you know that people search using the phrase "widgets in Southampton" then make that the name of your board.

You then need to make sure you have plenty of great content in the board which get lots of Likes and Re-pins. Getting Likes and Re-pins is not covered here, but a very quick and simple task should be to make sure you have your boards named correctly.

Below is an image of what has been returned by Google when searching "Great Garden Ideas" you will note that the top three unpaid links are all Pinterest. This has worked because the boards contain the phrase "Great Garden Ideas".

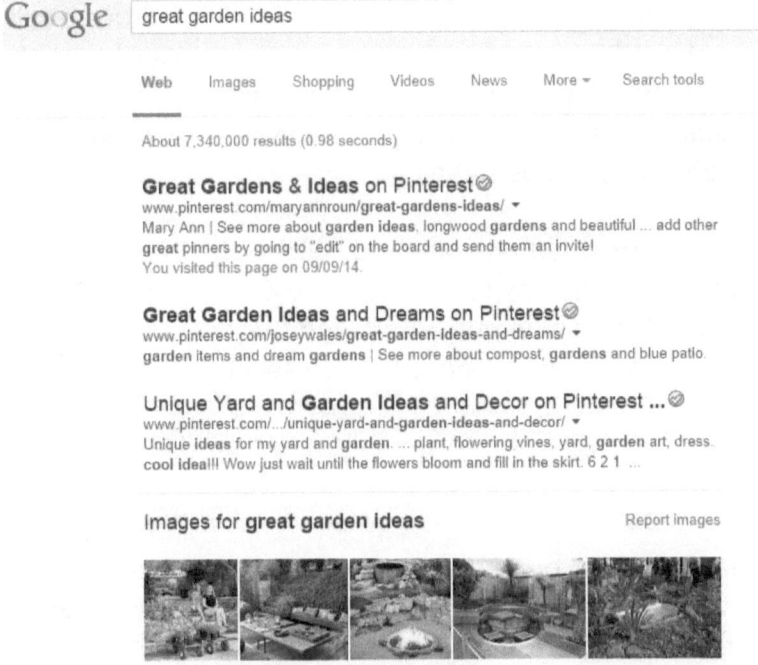

If you are new to Pinterest, this social media platform allows you to create visual posts (with descriptions) that you can assign to what are known as boards.

You can, for example, create a range of posts with different types of a product and 'pin' them to a board called 'Products'.

A clothes retailer might have a board called 'dresses' with a range of types and styles of dresses as well as another board called 'hats' with different types of... you've got... hats.

72. Make sure your pins have links on Pinterest

When you upload an image to Pinterest it is possible to have a URL pointing to the original source. This is a feature I really love about Pinterest which is not currently available in the same way on platforms such as Instagram, Facebook or LinkedIn. Frustratingly, Instagram doesn't allow you to add clickable links in posts at all.

With Pinterest, when somebody clicks on the image they can be taken directly to your website or online store where your product can be purchased, and this helps massively to increase conversions from a post on social media to a sale.

73. Use dlvr.it to make Pinterest posts more visual on other platforms

When you post on Pinterest there is a little checkbox that allows you to post onto Twitter or Facebook as well, which saves time, but to be honest the posts on Facebook and Twitter do not look very good and there is always a risk of chopping words off on Twitter midsentence (due to the character limit) which not only looks horrible but is also unprofessional.

Using a tool such as dlvr.it (https://dlvrit.com) means that when you make a post on Pinterest, it will pull the photo or image through to Facebook and the post will look a lot better.

This not only makes the post look a lot better, but it saves time compared to uploading images manually on Twitter and Facebook as well. It takes 5 to 10 minutes to set up your dlvr.it account and create a posting route from Pinterest to Twitter or Facebook. There is also a free account, so you don't have to pay any fees.

Make sure when doing this that you have the checkbox unchecked for posting to Twitter and Facebook, otherwise you risk posting the same Pinterest post on Twitter and Facebook twice... and only one of them will look good!

74. Invite people to pin to your board on Pinterest

Pinterest has a great feature which allows you to invite other people to pin on one (or more) of your boards.

If you provide information on local services, then you may invite a local museum or events host (such as a village hall or hotel) to pin updates.

You can save a lot of time sourcing and creating content whilst building relationships with partners. Their pins will be promoted and more visible as your number of followers grow and they are likely to keep on posting content for you.

Pinterest allows you to send a message to followers by dropping a pin into the message.

The idea behind this is that if you see a brilliant pin that you love and you know someone else who would like it then you can send them a message with the pin attached.

This can also be used to let people know about a new product or special offer you have. And it gets better... You can also include multiple people in the same message so that you don't have to keep sending the same message over and over again to reach a number of people.

A good use for this is to send people a coupon with money off or an image of a new product that you have launched to let them know it is now available.

Chapter 12: TikTok

TikTok has been growing massively in the last few years and even if you don't like creating silly or fun videos, it's important that you build your presence on this growing platform.

If you are in any doubts as to how effective it is, I know an accountant who has acquired 3 new clients within 6 months of setting up a TikTok account and posting on it.

There are various ways you can generate business on TikTok from posting your own content with offers and updates to interacting with your customers. Here are some ideas for growing your brand, and your sales, on TikTok.

76. Create 60 second video tips

When it comes to attracting and teaching (the AT in the ATM content model discussed earlier), there's no better way than creating short video tips on TikTok.

TikTok uses a different algorithm to Facebook and other platforms that's geared toward promoting visibility of content.

If you create a short video with 1 or 2 quick tips then TikTok will effectively promote it for you – giving you the opportunity to reach (or attract) as many people as possible that you can use your video to teach (or educate).

You might find it difficult to get enough information in with only 60 seconds but try your best! Going over 60 seconds seems to have an impact on visibility and the longer the video, the harder it is to keep the attention of anyone watching the video.

I also recommend posting the same video to Instagram.

77. Use TikTok's editing tools

TikTok has some amazing, and free editing features which you can use to create videos for other platforms such as Instagram or Twitter.

This allows you to add titles, sound effects, transition effects, fun stickers, backgrounds and even music.

If you are stuck for video ideas for other social platforms, consider creating something in TikTok that you can use on all of your platforms.

78. Create a video from gallery using music

If you don't want to record yourself, or other people, then you can always upload pictures from the gallery area on your phone.

Add a few special effects such as transitioning between pictures and some music and hey presto! You have a fun or promotional video that you can use to go viral on TikTok.

79. Promote your products with a quick video

If you have a product that sells better when people see how it works or what it looks like then why not create a quick video discussing what the product is, it's features and how it can help your customer?

80. Work with influencers

There are a fairly large number of high-profile influencers on TikTok and the concept of using influencers on social media is an established practice, mostly thanks to Instagram.

Using TikTok influencers, you can get them to review your products or simply mention it in one of their videos.

81. Focus on educational content

I know we have talked quite a bit about teaching or educating people with content such as tips but it's worth an extra mention with TikTok.

TikTok has become known for providing educational content whether it's how to fix a leaky tap to the vast range of recipe ideas that are on the platform.

I've maybe got a little bit carried away myself following profiles that give clever tips for doing math equations and learning Chinese!

If you provide food-related products or services, for example, then why not create your own educational series of posts that can go viral?

82. Use TikTok shopping

TikTok knows that a large number of products are being sold after being shown on their platform.

With this in mind, they have launched the ability to create your own shop for physical products.

If you run a store or an eCommerce business, I recommend setting up a TikTok shop.

Chapter 13: Blogging

Strictly speaking, you could argue that blogging isn't social media – and I tend to agree.

I've heard people say that social media is about interacting and is user generated content, and since you can add comments to blogs then it's a form of social media.

I'm not convinced, but I do want to share a couple of quick tips that involve blogging as they are linked to social media and some of the concepts around content that we have been discussing. Here they are…

83. Blog your way to higher credibility and trust

You only have 280 characters to get your message across on Twitter, and while other social media channels allow you to write longer content, it's well-known and proven that long wordy posts are less engaging (or eventually lose the interest of followers).

If, for example, your business offers wedding planning then there is no better way to show people that you know what you're talking about than writing a blog with the headline "15 great ways to make sure your wedding runs smoothly" or "A 75-point checklist for a successful wedding day".

There is no way you'd get all of this into a 280-character post on Twitter, but what you can do is use social media platforms to find your target market and then drive them to your website or blog where they can read up on your advice and opinions.

Write expert and informative content on your website or blog and use short, intriguing posts on social media to drive traffic to the site instead.

You can also do single posts on social media for each top tip with a link to your blog so that they can find out more.

84. Post blogs on groups

Posting old and new blogs on relevant Facebook and LinkedIn groups is a good way to drive potential customers to your site.

Find a group where your target market is present, find a relevant blog you have written (or write one) and post it on that group. Remember also to make sure to word the post so that you are seen as adding value to the group members and helping them out.

It's worth noting that if you don't have a large amount of social media presence then this can help reach much more people in a shorter period of time.

Your Facebook page might have 500 Likes, of which only a small percentage of people will see what you post on it but there are plenty of Facebook Groups with thousands of members and a large majority of them will see what you have posted.

85. Comment on other people's blogs

Positive comments on someone's blog post helps to raise awareness of who you are and what you offer. It also helps to start or build a relationship with them.

Simply, find a blog post of a potential customer, read it and comment on it, thanking them for the great insight and telling them how much you liked it.

Chapter 14: Messaging Apps

Most social media platforms allow you to message fans and contacts. LinkedIn and Facebook allow you to send a personal message while Instagram and Twitter allow you send a direct message (or DM for short).

All of these are similar but, in this chapter, I want to cover apps that are predominantly focused on message one to one or one to group.

Platforms such as Instagram have a core focus on content posting rather than messaging.

Messaging apps include WhatsApp and SMS text messaging, although out of the two of these, it seems like WhatsApp has become the default messaging solution!

Here are some ideas for using messaging apps to grow your business:

86. Set up a WhatsApp group for tips and updates

Whether it's part of the prospecting process or building loyalty with existing customers, a WhatsApp group where members can receive tips and updates is a great way to stay connected with them.

With prospecting, a good way to do this is to offer a 5-day challenge that includes access to a WhatsApp group. A personal trainer, for example, can create a 5-day challenge such as "cut out sugar from your diet in just 5 days" that includes a workbook and motivational tips via WhatsApp.

87. Use messaging to chase leads

Currently, messaging is highly effective as it gets a much higher response rate than some other forms of marketing.

If a customer expresses an interest in an upcoming event you are hosting, or abandons their shopping cart on your website, then you can chase them up with a friendly WhatsApp message.

88. Add WhatsApp to your website

Chat bots have their advantages, but if you want potential customers to get hold of you easily then adding a WhatsApp widget is a great way to make buying and getting in touch easier.

Adding this to your website means that someone can instantly call or message you from your website using WhatsApp.

Chapter 15: Other Platforms

89. Track questions on Quora related to your services

Quora is a social media platform where people ask questions, and anybody can respond to them. Questions fall into various categories, and you can also follow these categories.

For example, if you sell a product designed to help businesses improve their customer experience then you can follow the categories labelled customer experience or customer service.

There are a lot of people asking questions such as "how can I improve the customer service in my hotel" or "what's the best way to improve customer service when talking to customers on the phone". Giving great advice to these people will get you credibility with people who have clearly shown they have a need for your services.

Take 20 minutes to set up a Quora account, to follow some relevant categories and respond to 1 or 2 questions.

90. Track questions on Reddit related to your service

Reddit is a direct competitor of Quora and it's a great forum for asking and answering questions.

Simply sign up for an account and then search for questions based on keywords related to your service or area of expertise.

Even if you only spend 10 minutes a week searching on Reddit and really help someone by answering a question which you can add value then you are gaining exposure and positioning yourself as an expert.

People are more likely to pay attention to experienced advice and this could lead to a sale.

91. Use Clubhouse

If you aren't familiar with Clubhouse, it's an app that allows you to join live audio discussions. You can join a discussion around all sorts of topics such as best marketing practices, tips for bookkeeping, how to meditate and so on.

A great way to engage with and educate your audience about what you do is to set up a profile on Clubhouse and then have live discussions with your target audience as well as other experts in your field.

92. Snapchat a sneaky product preview

Snapchat really took off amongst teenagers a few years back and, although it has stalled somewhat, it's still popular among teens.

So how does it work?

Basically, you take a picture on your phone and send it to one or many of your friends. The image can then only be viewed by the people who receive it for only a few seconds.

You can also create what is called a story, which allows you to mesh images together to run one after the other to create a story.

So how can you use it in your business? Well, if you are launching a product or opening a new store, then you could create a teaser campaign and encourage people to follow you on Snapchat.

Users can be enticed to follow you by letting them know you will be giving previews of your new product or store exclusive to Snapchat users. This helps to grow your followers on Snapchat as well as increasing the interactions with your audience.

93. Snapchat a discount code

Snapchat (see previous tip for explanation on what Snapchat is) can be used to send an image of a discount code that followers can use online. With social media platforms such as Twitter and Facebook your posts can easily be missed by some of your audience due to the high volume of content that goes through these platforms, but this is less of a problem with Snapchat.

Receiving an image post through Snapchat is a bit like receiving a text message. You are very unlikely to miss it and you will treat it as important. Simply post an image of a discount code to your followers and make sure to include an expiry date that is in the near future.

94. Capture leads with YouTube

To do this you need to have video content either already posted, or ready to upload to YouTube. There are two elements to this tip: the right wording and including a call to action.

The biggest mistake people make on YouTube is to leave the title or description blank or badly worded. If you provide cleaning services and do a video on how to clean wine out of a carpet then people will search with keywords words such as 'clean up', 'remove' and 'wine'. Your video will not be found based on what you say in the video.

YouTube uses the written words in the title and description to determine what your video is about so a description saying, "Here is how to remove wine stains out of a carpet" is more likely to appear in search results when people type 'how to remove wine stains out of a carpet".

The next element in this tip is the call to action. Once someone has found you and watched the video, they should get in touch to let the professionals help them out. You can add a call to action in your video when you upload it to YouTube.

Also, by including a URL or other contact details in the description, viewers can contact you immediately, and this is much more effective than them simply subscribing to your YouTube channel.

Make sure to include a call to action that is of benefit to anyone who sees it - and make sure the call to action is the first few lines of the description so they don't have to click "read more" to see it.

A strong call to action in the above example may be a free guide with 7 steps to keeping your carpet clean. When they click on the link, they will be taken to a landing page where they must enter their telephone and email address.

Now you have a profile of someone who has searched for how to remove wine from a carpet, watched the video and downloaded the guide. Prospects don't get much hotter than that, and you have their contact details ready to get in touch. I guess you know what the next step would be!

95. Set up and post weekly on Google My Business

Google My Business (or GMB for short) isn't truly a social media platform like LinkedIn or Instagram. You can post on it, and you can leave reviews and ask questions, but it's not set up for social interactions like the main platforms.

In reality, GMB is focused on other areas such as appearing in search results and promoting local businesses who can also be found on Google Maps.

If you run a local business, I recommend setting up a Google My Business profile and posting an image once a week.

This helps with being found on Google and it also entices customers to your location.

If you are a restaurant or café for example, then posting weekly specials or your weekly menu is a great way to tickle the taste buds of your target audience!

96. Get reviews on Google My business

Getting reviews from customers is without doubt a powerful marketing tool and one of the great features of Google My Business is the ability to have your business reviewed – and for those reviews to be visible in search results.

Of course, this only applies if you have positive 4 and 5-star reviews.

If someone searches for what you offer on Google Search and a number of GMB profiles appear, which one would you opt to buy from, the profile with no reviews or the profile with 200 reviews averaging 4.5 stars?

If you encourage customers to leave you a review then you are more likely to get found and customers are more likely to buy from you.

This also comes with an added bonus. Reviews can be used on platforms such as Facebook and Instagram. You can take the wording from the review and either paste it into a post or, for a more visual impact, create an image with the wording in the image.

Here's a free template on Stencil that you can use:

https://bit.ly/36mCNAW

You can easily change the wording before clicking on Save and then the Download button.

If you would like to know more about using Google My Business, you might be interested in my book Getting to the Top of Google.

Chapter 16: Prospecting

Whether via social media or in person, building your relationships is a long-term process, and the ultimate goal is to strengthen your network, one person at a time. ~ Raymond Arroyo

Posting content is great! And it's easy to spend all day on social media writing engaging posts and even interacting with people who might not be a relevant prospect, but there is a lot more you can do to grow your business.

A good way to find new business is to interact with prospects that you can turn into customers, as well as to interact with customers that you want to build a relationship with over the long-term.

There is nothing wrong with interacting with people all day, providing they are the right people, and you are making money and generating healthy leads that justify the time and effort.

In the next chapter, we will focus more on long-term relationship building and building trust. In this chapter, we are focused more on direct prospecting and there's a lot to cover!

Below are some quick and easy ways to prospect and find customers. First of all, let's discuss strategy...

Prospecting, posting and other activities on social media can be daunting but if you have a strategy and plan of action with activities broken down then that can really help.

It helps by providing clarity and reducing overwhelm ("where do I start?").

I recommend going through the steps of deciding which platforms you will prospect on then create 1-3 daily actions that you will to to find new customers.

The activities you do will become more apparent as you read through this chapter of the book.

FREE Strategy Template!

You can download your free Prospecting Strategy template and fill it in as you go through the rest of this book!

Use the link below to grab a copy:

https://social.darrenhignett.com/prospectingstrategy

Remember to save a copy so that you can edit the template.

You might wonder why you want to follow your customers when you are prospecting. There are a couple of main reasons for this. First of all, it will help you understand your customers better.

Since your customers know who you are (and if they don't then you have a slightly different problem to address!) they are likely to follow you back and will then see your newsfeed and what you post.

One of the easiest ways to grow your business is to increase the number of sales with existing customers.

It may be that they are only aware of the basic product and didn't know about some of the services that you already provide and by following you on social media they will now get to understand your brand better as well as get to know some other products that they either didn't know about or were not sure about purchasing previously.

The other benefit of this approach is that your customers should be the biggest ambassadors of your product.

They are more likely to interact and share your posts and if they have friends and followers who are also potential customers then they are effectively spreading the word for you via social media - and very possibly spreading the word to your ideal target market. If you are in a particular trade, then your customers will be connected to colleagues and business contacts that they know from the same trade.

A great way to quickly find your customers or contacts on Twitter is to import your contacts list.

Twitter then searches the email addresses against registered users and returns a list of people that it has found. With just a few clicks you can quickly follow all the profiles it has matched.

99. Like what your prospects do

It's not always ideal to share the content of what your prospects do. It may be something you like but it's still not appropriate to your audience. Added to this, Instagram doesn't allow you to share posts unless it's sent via a direct message to individuals.

An easier and quicker way to acknowledge the content of other people is to Like what they have done.

On Pinterest, you may search for a topic that will return the pins from people you want to interact with. You can then look at those pins and Like the ones that you not only like, but they have also been posted by people you want to do business with.

Note: be careful in your approach when doing this. I do not recommend clicking Like for a load of pins en masse just to get attention.

Your profile will appear with the huge amount of Likes that possibly make no sense when people view your profile, and you may easily come across as someone who is liking everything randomly to drum up attention.

What I'm talking about here is a targeted activity used selectively. Where appropriate, you might want to comment on posts as well.

Top Tip: Put 5 minutes aside every day or 2 days to review your prospects and contacts on LinkedIn, Instagram or Twitter and Like or comment on any posts that you genuinely like. Don't use the 5 minutes to randomly scroll through your newsfeed. Use the time wisely with a focus on Liking and commenting. You might also want to share as well.

100. Find and refer on social media

It's always difficult when prospecting on social media to make sure that you're not too pushy and too promotional but here is a clever idea. Rather than look for customers interested in buying your services, you could look for somebody interested in one of your prospect's services.

Why would you do this? Surely that sounds like a strange thing to do but bear with me.

Let's take an example.

If a person on Twitter (who you may want to do business with) asks if anybody knows a good accountant, then you could recommend your own accountant or an accountant that you have met at a networking event.

By doing this, you are adding value to the person who is asking the question as well as really getting yourself in the good books of the accountant that you recommended (no pun intended by using good books and accountant in the same sentence).

In five minutes, you have managed to grab the attention and appreciation of two potential prospects.

You have not annoyed and frustrated anybody by directly selling your services and I'm sure that if you want to talk to them at a later date about your services then they will always be happy to speak to "the really helpful guy on social media who seems really nice and gave me some help with an issue I had once".

You can do this kind of referral on Twitter and Instagram as well as on question forums such as LinkedIn groups. Reddit and Quora should also be considered but be conscious of the fact that these platforms may require that you explain your affiliation with the people you are recommending.

Try spending 10 minutes every week to recommend someone on social media that you trust.

Found a great article that someone else has written? Post it and mention them in the post. Want to thank people for their support during the week or at the end of the day? Create a thank you post and mention them.

Mentioning people on social media helps to build on the relationship with them and it brings you and your business to the front of their mind. When you mention people on platforms such as LinkedIn, the person you mention will be notified by email as well as a message appearing in the notifications area that you have mentioned them.

People who are mentioned are more likely to comment, share or like the post, increasing your exposure online further. It's worth noting that if you mention too many people, too often then it might impact how other people see your posts.

Seeing posts every day that thank a bunch of people you don't know doesn't add value if you aren't involved in the activity but doing it from time to time and being conscious of others, is a highly effective way of getting interactions and building relationships.

Here are some examples of how you can mention others:

It was great to see ABC and DEF today, thanks for your time!
Here's a great article by ABC
Some top tips on getting better results. Maybe this is of use ABC?

Remember to use the @ symbol when naming someone so that they are tagged properly and are notified by the social media platform.

102. Use a SocialCRM tool to track opportunities and get closer to your prospects

On average, sales and marketing costs average from 15%-35% of total corporate costs. So, the effort to automate for more sales efficiency is absolutely essential. In cases reviewed, sales increase due to advanced CRM technology have ranged from 10% to more than 30%. ~ Harvard Business Review

Using a CRM (short for customer relationship management) application is an absolute must as part of any sales process and CRM tools have evolved considerably in the last 10 years to help you manage and track opportunities for social media.

With so much activity and so many conversations taking place on social media it's easy to forget who a potential customer might be, who you spoke to and very easy to forget that you need to stay in contact with certain individuals to build up the relationship and trust with them.

This is where SocialCRM comes in. Tools such as Nimble will import your social media contacts and display reminders on when you should get back in touch with them.

Viewing a particular contact's profile will also allow you to see what they are posting on the various social media channels that you are connected to them on.

This is ideal for helping you to interact with prospects on a personal level. It also helps having that information at hand if you need to talk to them over the phone or email them.

Besides Nimble, there are many other CRM tools available that allow you to include social media activity in your sales and marketing tracking. If you don't currently use a CRM, below are some names you may want to take a look at.

Salesforce
Microsoft Dynamics
Zoho CRM
Sprout Social
HubSpot CRM

There are many more CRM tools and which one you chose depends on your budget, how much social media integration you intend to have and your business processes. Whichever one you select – make sure to you use it to its potential.

103. Integrate face to face with online connections

If you have just had a meeting with someone, stay connected and build trust and the relationship with them by connecting with them on LinkedIn and by Liking their Facebook page (assuming that they are on both of these platforms!).

You could go the full distance and follow them on Instagram and other platforms as well, but it might come across as being a bit creepy. Having said that, following their Instagram business or Twitter profile a few weeks later is ok.

It's important to connect with them on at least one platform within 48 hours of meeting them, while your meeting with them is fresh on their mind. It helps to keep the momentum in building up the relationship.

104. Keep the conversation going (but don't be annoying)

So, someone has said, thanks for following or connecting, what next? Most people don't respond, and the relationship stops there but it makes a huge difference if you quickly reply to a contact by showing an interest in them or their business.

If a user is in the 'widget' industry thanks you for a great post you have done, or for following then it takes only a minute or two to respond with something like: "you are welcome, how is the sales of widgets this time of year?"?

The first thought is "wow, this person has checked out my profile and sees that I am in the industry of selling widgets. They are also showing an interest in what I do". Keeping the conversation going increases the number of interactions and the likelihood that they will buy from you in the future.

A good way to keep the conversation going is by asking a question. Try to avoid low value questions such as "How is the weather in your area?" or "How is your day going?" Try to strike up a conversation of value that shows an interest in them.

Also be careful not to go too far. Asking too many questions can feel like you are stalking or trying too hard. Conversations often come to a natural ending and that's ok. You may need to change tact by liking or sharing their posts or even suggesting a meeting or phone call to discuss working together.

105. Connect after a face to face meet up

This is one of the simplest, easiest and yet often not done marketing activities.

You attend a networking event or meeting with a potential customer and return to the office with a business card (which you then bury in your desk rubble only to risk it finally ending up in the bin!) and you carry on with business as normal.

If you could just take 2 minutes of your time to connect with them on LinkedIn – and possibly Like a post they have done, then this will hugely increase the effectiveness of the meeting you have had - and will increase the number of 'touch points' with the client that may buy from you.

If you can spare an extra couple of minutes, then you may even want to mention them on social media and say how good it was to meet them. This is of course assuming that you are okay to publicly mention someone when your competitors may be watching.

Personally, I don't see anything wrong with that as you have now started to build a strong relationship with a potential new client and the pros outweigh the cons but in larger companies, this might be a bigger concern.

Spend just 3-5 minutes after meeting up to connect with that person in some way on social media. It is a small amount of effort that could potentially make the difference when getting a sale.

106. Move a prospective chat to LinkedIn

It's not always ideal when you gain a new follower on a social media platform to drive them to another, but in this case, it can work very well. If you deal business to business (or B2B) then you can sometimes find customers easier on Twitter or possibly Instagram and start the conversation.

Once you have established contact you can take it to the next level by inviting the contact to connect on LinkedIn.

This not only allows you to take the conversation beyond 280 characters, but it also allows the prospect to see your profile and your skill sets using a more business focused platform. Adding someone as a connection on LinkedIn tends to feel more powerful than using Twitter.

If you have had a good initial chat or number of interactions on Twitter with a potential prospect, then look them up on LinkedIn and invite them to connect. Remember to personalise your message and even include that you have been talking on Twitter. There is a greater chance they will remember you and accept your invitation.

107. Warm up your sales call or letter

Social media presents an opportunity for businesspeople to connect and know each other prior to a phone call or email taking place. ~ Jeffrey Gitomer

Cold calling... you either love it or you hate it (with most people hating it). Personally, I don't like receiving cold calls and I don't like making them, but I have no problem with picking up the phone and talking to someone after a few conversations or interactions online.

The recipient of the phone call or letter will be much more responsive if you have followed them on Twitter or joined in a conversation in a LinkedIn group that they are also participating in.

A short activity like this should take very little time and only needs to be done a few days before making the call and will increase the chances of converting the sales call or letter into a sale.

If you have already established contact with someone then it's always good to interact with them on social media to help build and reinforce the relationship.

If you have just had a meeting with a potential customer, then take 5 minutes to check out their profile on social media and see if you can interact in some way.

If they have just posted an interesting article on LinkedIn for example, then you may want to share it or comment on it.

This particularly applies to any business that has a fixed location visited by customers. If you are on a high street with a high footfall, then offering details in your window of where people can find you on social media will help build long-term relationships.

It is also especially useful during hours when you may be closed! They may not be able to visit you, but they can still connect with you on social media when they see the details in your front window.

If you want to really show off your high-tech credentials you can also include signs that use NFC and QR codes to make it easier to connect. People passing by a shop or restaurant can then quickly connect on social media with their mobile phone.

With regards to QR codes and NCF, if you're not sure what I'm talking about here is a quick explanation:

QR codes are barcodes which you can scan with the camera on your mobile phone. When a passer-by scans the QR code in the window they are redirected on their mobile phone immediately to your Twitter, Facebook, or Instagram account.

NFC is a relatively newer technology which involves touching the sign in the window with your phone. Once contact is made the mobile phone will automatically open up the social media profile for the user to connect with.

110. Free Wi-Fi for a Like or Follow

If you are a hotel or restaurant, you may already be offering free Wi-Fi to your visitors. They may need to enter their email address which is great – especially if your marketing plan includes email marketing to those visitors to entice them back.

There is, however, an easier and equally effective alternative – allowing people to connect to the Wi-Fi for free once they have Liked your page on Facebook or followed you on Twitter.

Offering Free Wi-fi for a Like is easier for the visitor than filling in a form and is more acceptable than having to declare their email address.

It could be even easier for the customer by offering the Wi-Fi for free with no login but if you want to build loyalty with customers and stay in contact then a smart idea would be to capture their email address or get them to Like or follow you on social media in exchange for accessing your Wi-Fi.

This seems a perfectly acceptable request to your customers providing it is as hassle free as possible (note I mentioned earlier that one of the biggest reasons for shopping cart abandonment is the frustration of having to register).

There are Wi-Fi access points available to buy which include this functionality. If you are a hotel with a restaurant that gets 20 new visitors a day, then a simple calculation shows that you will have 7,300 new Facebook Likes over the year (based on 365 days a year).

That's 7,300 people who have visited your venue and that you can now market to on an ongoing basis to attract them back for repeat business.

It's important to balance this with the idea of doing email marketing. It's proven that email marketing can be more effective than using social media, but it does require more effort creating email marketing campaigns as well as more effort for customers having to sign in.

Either way, using Wi-Fi to help you interact through email marketing or social media are both great ways to grow your business.

The ideal scenario here is that you write an article demonstrating to your target market how they can benefit from the type of services you offer (in a none too promotional way).

You then post the link to your article on a platform such as LinkedIn or Twitter, mentioning someone who may find your article of interest and is, of course, a potential customer. They find it useful, and you have introduced yourself to a potential new client who you can now start building a strong relationship with.

For example, imagine you provide email marketing services to the health and fitness sector. You may write an article with 10 tips on how fitness instructors can target people who want to become healthier.

Then write a social media post to a fitness instructor that says "Hey @fitness instructor. Here are 10 ways to help market to the health-conscious customer" – and add the link.

If you have already written a blog or article, then fantastic. I appreciate it takes time to write articles and if you don't have the time to do this then the next best alternative is to find a third-party article that you could send to them providing of course that it is not your direct competitor!

You can also use services such as Fiverr (www.fiverr.com) to have your blog written in its basic format for only $5, saving you at least an hour of work.

112. Tag customers and contacts

Instagram, LinkedIn and Twitter allow you to tag people in the images or words that you post, and this will then be brought to the attention of the people that you tag.

If the services that you offer involve events such as training or seminars where you meet with your customers, then you can tag them in images you post from the event.

Posting images of the events demonstrates on social media the kind of activity that you do in a highly visual way to your followers and there is a high possibility that your customers will interact or share your posts.

This form of interaction helps to build the relationship with existing customers over the long-term as well as enticing them to share the content with their followers who are potential new clients to you as well.

113. Research before calling or emailing

Using social media, you can quickly check out the profiles of the person in the company that you are about to send an email to or call.

If you are prospecting, then this can make a huge difference to the way you approach the next step and will increase your chances of conversion.

Just make sure not to be too spooky or scary in the way you research you do or what you say! If you happen to see they went out for a beer on Saturday night on Facebook, then you probably don't want to ask questions about it or mention it unless they bring it up first.

The type of information I am talking about using to your advantage may be if their business profile says that they are growing fast or having success in a particular sector.

If they have just promoted their attendance at an exhibition, then you may want to ask how it went and if it was busy. This kind of conversation helps to warm up the prospect to you and it shows you have an interest in them and care.

114. Offering a free e-book, training event or trial

So far in this book I have talked a lot about integrating social media with other channels of marketing such as emails, phone calls and blogging, but I haven't talked much about integrating it with offers or a strong call to action.

Great content is important, and people will appreciate it, but it doesn't always drive the customer to buy immediately. If you have written an e-book or white paper, then rather than just posting a link to it, or giving it away completely free you may want to have the condition that they provide you with an email address or telephone number so that you can establish contact with them.

You may want to offer a training event with the chance to meet up with people face-to-face or a limited trial so that customers can try your services. This helps build confidence in what you offer before they make a commitment.

All these call to actions encourage interactions with people who have an interest in your product.

They may not be ready to buy right now so having those details will help you to stay in touch. In many cases the customer may not think that they are ready to buy but after reading the free e-book or attending the training event they may realise how beneficial your services are.

The call to action such as an e-book or training event doesn't have to be free. It could be discounted.

What's important is that you promote it with a call to action and capture a way of establishing contact such as an email address.

115. Import your email address book

Most social media platforms are constantly nagging you to import your contacts and it's a great idea.

If you have an email address book of people you interact with regularly, or even people you have been in contact with in the last 12 months then following them on social media is a great way to strengthen the relationship with them.

Rather than spend time looking for people to interact with on social media, you have a ready-made list of people who are familiar with you and are likely to follow back.

This really is a quick and effective way to grow your followers in the initial stages.

Spend just 5 minutes on one or two social media platforms to import your contacts and follow them.

116. Direct message your existing followers

Once you have an established number of followers on a platform such as Instagram, Twitter, TikTok or LinkedIn with posts going out regularly, you may want to send a select few of them a message offering a promotion that you are running.

It's highly recommended that you do this only when you have built up trust with your followers and that you don't do it too often.

Think carefully about the wording and who you are targeting. You may for example only want to send a message to those in London and have been interacting with you.

This activity should only take 10 to 15 minutes once you have decided what the wording and the promotion is that you would like to offer.

You might be wondering why this isn't in the chapter for LinkedIn, or if it isn't a repeat of the previous point. The power of using LinkedIn direct messages is powerful enough that I feel it merits being separated and being placed under the chapter on prospecting.

Sending a private message to someone on LinkedIn can get a very good response, providing it is worded correctly. The response rate to messages on LinkedIn is higher than the open rate on emails when sending out a marketing campaign.

There are two ways to use LinkedIn messaging effectively. If you have a good number of connections already that are relevant, then you can simply message them.

Alternatively, you can send a direct message to members of a LinkedIn group that you are a member of.

So, if you have joined a LinkedIn group full of potential clients that would love to talk to you then you can quickly go down the list and select the potential contacts you believe most appropriate and then send them a personal message.

LinkedIn members on a paid subscription can also message people directly without having to join a group.

Chapter 17: Building Trust

Increasingly, consumers don't search for products and services. Rather, services come to their attention via social media. ~ Erik Qualman

Lots of the tactics we have covered so far have been on building trust as well as demonstrating your expertise and educating/teaching the prospect about what you do.

Trust, demonstrating expertise and teaching all work together in a powerful way – and this model applies to all levels of marketing, not just when using social media.

In this chapter, I have included some extra ways to build trust that don't really fit in the prospecting chapter.

118. Build strategic relationships

People influence people. Nothing influences people more than a recommendation from a trusted friend. A trusted referral influences people more than the best broadcast message. A trusted referral is the Holy Grail of advertising. ~ Mark Zuckerberg

Not all your effort has to be on directly prospecting and looking for customers. In fact, a large part of it may be focused on the indirect approach of building strong relationships with partners and people who can refer you.

I have had many contacts refer business to me who I have met on Twitter after interacting with them and this approach can be invaluable.

People in the industry – or similar industries – may have clients with needs that they cannot fulfil. A bakery offering wedding cakes may be a good person to a refer customers if you are a photographer, florist, or wedding dress maker.

By talking to these contacts on social media and building up relationships you could have a steady stream of customers who already have trust in you because you have been recommended.

Try connecting, sharing and interacting with one or two strategic partners every week. It should only be 5 to 10 minutes of your time and if one partner leads to a good order then time has certainly not been wasted.

119. Hang-out with prospects and promote your offering

During the pandemic, there was a huge rise in the number of people hosting or taking part in webinars. With lockdown, there wasn't much we could do, and we couldn't go out, so webinars became the trend.

Very quickly, webinar fatigue set in, and the wonders of webinar wore off.

Today, webinars are still effective as a marketing tool (think Teach in the ATM model), but they do have one drawback: They aren't the most personal of ways to talk to your target audience and it's not really geared to interacting with attendees.

You can do audiocasts such as podcasts, Twitter Spaces and Clubhouse (see previous tactics for more on these), but you can also go visual with live video.

Live video streaming is a great way to put a face to the business. Prospects can see who you are. They can become familiar with you and can see how great you would be to deal with. This is especially important for service-based businesses such as coaches, accountants and trainers.

With most apps, you can set up an event and then invite people to attend. You then get a dedicated 30 to 60 minutes of your prospects time.

You should also consider a special offer for anyone who attends. This not only entices people to attend and listen, it also acts as a strong call to action to make your video call more effective for your business.

120. Target influencers

I have talked a lot about prospecting directly or through a connection but there is another way to reach more potential customers.

With a bit of research, you can find people on LinkedIn, Instagram and Twitter that have a high number of connections and are established in your line of business.

If they don't compete with you, you might want to work with them and form a partnership that costs nothing and that helps you to promote each other.

Alternatively, you can mention them in social media posts and interact with them, increasing the chances that they will either share your content or endorse you publicly in some way.

Influencers have already built up a high level of trust with their target audience. So much in fact that their audience is often desperate to join their future live streams and suffer FOMO (fear of missing out) if they don't catch their latest social media post.

Top Tip: Spend just 20 minutes working out who you can partner with mutually online and who the top influencers are that you can interact with. Then, put a few minutes aside every week to interact with them in the appropriate way.

Chapter 18: Running Campaigns

In this chapter, there are some ideas for campaigns that you can run.

121. Run an Amazon or eBay promotion on social media

If you sell products online using Amazon, eBay or Etsy for example, then you absolutely should be running campaigns regularly to attract more customers, and there is no better way to communicate your promotions than using a mixture of email marketing and social media.

Below are some examples of what you could do:

Set up a coupon code on Amazon and then send a direct message on Twitter to your followers to let them know about the discount code. You could also make it clear that it is a promotion only for Twitter followers as a thank you for following you on social media.

If your average sale price on eBay is £25 then offer money off any purchases over £40 with the aim of upselling a customer from purchasing one to two items. Then send an email and post on social media to your audience to let them know about the promotion and the fact that they need to act now as there are only 48 hours left.

Setting up a campaign on Amazon or eBay takes less than 10 minutes to do.

We have talked previously about using Facebook Ads and email marketing in competitions but what we are talking about here is the use of Facebook Ads to grow your email distribution list.

In other words, we are not using advertising on social media to grow social media presence, we are using it to grow our email marketing effectiveness.

Growing your email marketing list with relevant people who are genuinely interested in receiving your emails can take time.

Using a Facebook Ads campaign to direct people to sign up to a free newsletter means you can quickly reach out to a very large audience and capture the contact details of people who are genuinely interested in what you offer.

There are alternative ways to use Facebook Ads, such as to directly sell your product and bring a quick sale or to grow your likes, but these both have pros and cons.

A direct sell strategy brings results, but it also risks alienating people who do not like being sold to straightaway. This audience wants to have a higher level of trust in your brand before purchasing, which an email campaign will help to do.

Put together correctly, a Facebook Ads campaign that reaches only your target market and with an irresistible call to action to receive something free (such as a white paper or voucher code) when they sign up will help you to quickly build your email list.

If you sell beauty products, for example, you may target females in a particular age group who have an interest in topics such as perfume or makeup.

123. Run a social media campaign with 'sign up' to win

In a nutshell, lots of people provide their email addresses with a chance of winning a prize. If the prize includes your services for free, then you will know that the people responding certainly have an interest in your product!

The net result will be that you gain plenty of email addresses to market to, and you only have to give away one prize (give away more if you want to but people don't enter a competition to win second prize).

You only need to offer a first prize of £100/$100 worth of goods and you may claim as many as 500 email addresses.

You could run the promotion by setting up a landing page with an entry form, and you can also use Facebook Ads to promote the competition.

The amount of email addresses you collect will depend on various factors such as how long the promotion runs for and how much you spend on an Ads campaign.

There are also various apps that you can use such as KingSumo. These apps can be used to capture an email address and offer some cool features such as allowing the entrant to increase their chances of winning by sharing on social media and through other channels.

Using an app like this helps your competition – and brand – to go viral!

124. Share or use a hashtag to win

There are two options here. The first one is to ask people to share your post to be entered into a competition to win.

Doing this means the end objective is to make your brand go viral by getting lots of people to share awareness of your promotion… and brand.

The second form of competition you can use is to ask people (particularly on Twitter) to post using a particular hashtag for a chance to win.

The posts could be testimonials about how great your product is, or it could be including a picture of your product. When other people on Twitter click on the hashtag in a post, they will see great endorsements or pictures of your products. Your audience has done a heap of marketing for you in exchange for one of them receiving a prize.

125. Flock to unlock

This kind of promotion is specific to Twitter, although the concept can be used differently for platforms such as Instagram or TikTok.

The concept is that the more people who sign up to something or retweet a post that you have done the better the deal.

For example, if 50 people retweet your promotional post then you could reveal a coupon with 50% off. The more people get involved and more viral the marketing, the better the deal for your customers - and of course it's better for you as well!

This campaign is heavily focused on viral marketing rather than directly converting a participant into a sale.

If 50 people Retweet to their 100+ followers, then you have gained a considerable amount of exposure with at least 5,000 people potentially seeing posts about your product or service!

126. Give to charity!

When it comes to social media, people love charities. The idea of supporting a charity with a Like or Share is extremely popular.

You could, for example, donate a small (or big) amount of money for every new follower or like that you gain.

You can also use other channels including email marketing and other social media platforms to promote your campaign. If you have budget available, a Twitter or Facebook ads campaign will also help to promote your campaign further.

Not only will you be growing your online presence with viral marketing, but you can put your mind at rest knowing you are giving to a good cause and making a difference in the world!

Chapter 19: Time Saving Tips

It's easy to spend hours on social media marketing, so here are some quick tips for being for efficient!

127. Limit your time

This sounds easy enough, but it isn't. There is plenty of research and articles that talk about how social media and mobile phones are designed to grab and keep our attention.

Here are some quick tips for limiting your time:

Set blocks of time that are dedicated to working on social media content or prospecting. For example: 2-4 pm every Friday is for content creation, and you will only check your social media feeds and prospect 3 times a day for half an hour (say 9 am, 1 pm and 3 pm).

Use an app such as the Facebook Newsfeed Eradicator (in the Google Chrome Browser store) to remove distractions that take up your time. This neat app replaces your newsfeed with an inspiration quote so that you can work on scheduling content without being distracted by what your brother, sister or aunt has posted.

Use a timer with an alarm. Set it for 25 minutes and tell yourself that the work you do on social media must be complete by then.

Knowing that you only have a limited time to work on social media means that the mind becomes more focused. You will get more done and will be much more effective as well as efficient!

128. Outsource or automate

If you do something repeatedly then it should be automated. This can save a huge amount of time which you can then use to focus on other business and marketing activities.

Content scheduling with the help of an app is something that can be automated.

Alternatively, if you don't have the time to manage your social media then I recommend outsourcing some or all of the activities.

You might want to use a digital marketing agency to create and schedule your core content while you do the prospecting – or you might want to outsource everything including marketing campaigns including Facebook Ads.

If you spend 4 hours a day on social media, what could you be doing with your time to grow your business if you outsourced that work and freed up those 4 hours a day?

And let's put that into perspective. 4 hours a day is 20 hours a week or 80+ hours a month!

129. Share from an app on your mobile during 'down time'

As brilliant, useful... and addictive... as mobile phones are, they are not the best of devices for writing and posting content (the term "fat fingers" is perfect for explaining when the wrong buttons are pressed, and your Instagram post goes out saying something you certainly didn't intend to say!).

There is a way around this if you have the right apps installed on your mobile.

Imagine this scenario, you arrive in a hotel lobby an hour early for your meeting. You don't have any reading materials and it's too much effort to power the laptop up to do anything, so you start playing with your mobile phone (sound familiar?).

You launch the BBC news app to see what's going on in the world and discover an article that is relevant to your followers.

Perfect! Now will you remember to share it later on in the evening when you get back home in front of your laptop?

Probably not, but if you click on the share button then you can very quickly share the content with the correct wording and URL.

It should only take a few minutes to do, and your followers will see that you are posting the latest and greatest current affairs related to what they are interested in.

130. Repeat good content (and content that works)

Once you have formulated content that people interact with and like then there is no harm in repeating it, providing that you do not repeat it too often and too frequently within a short period of time.

If you posted something on January 1st, then people are unlikely to remember four or five months later.

If content is repeated too frequently, people will notice and will lose interest in your newsfeed. You should also try to avoid repeating content that is news related such as current affairs.

There is no point in reinventing the wheel. Build up a list of posts you think could be repeated several times and make sure to track them in a spreadsheet.

Content can take a long time to put together on a daily or weekly basis so building up a log of good quality content that you know is effective and can save you a lot of time can really help you get results.

With Instagram, it's more noticeable to fans if you are repeating content with the same image as all of your recent posts can be seen together when visiting your profile.

For this reason, I suggest either using a different image or not repeating content on Instagram within a 6-month period.

Note: Twitter rules prevent you from repeating content that is exactly the same.

If, for example, you want to promote a service that you offer then I recommend creating different versions of the same post such as:

Check out this product...
Have you seen this...?
We are offering this product...
Why not try out...

The words above might not be the exact words you use, but you can see how variations of the same theme or post can be quickly put together in a spreadsheet and then posted on social media.

Chapter 20: The Integrated Approach

I would be crazy if I told you that social media is the only way to market your business. Although it's very important, like any other form of marketing, it needs to be used in conjunction with other activities and channels to make it work to its full potential.

Exhibiting at a trade show for example, will not be as effective if you don't email to your contacts and broadcast your attendance on social media – as well as follow up with leads using various marketing activities.

You may also for example want to use other marketing activities (such as radio advertising) to encourage people to connect with you on social media, and it may be the case that some of your customers don't use social media regularly (at least not yet) and for them, a combination of different marketing channels is required.

I've also worked with a business that warmed up sales calls by following them on Twitter first, while others have called businesses that have clicked on links in an email marketing campaign.

Taking an integrated approach improves the effectiveness of campaigns. Here are some ways you can integrate social media marketing with other activities:

131. Be social with your email Signature

The purpose of the email signature (besides complying with legislation) is to make it easy for people to get in touch with you outside of email if they need to.

If you are in email contact with a potential customer, then make sure to include your social media profiles so that they can connect with you very quickly and easily.

You may also want to use an app such as WiseStamp or EmailBadge. These apps allow you to make great looking email signatures that can include your social media links.

132. Keep customers App-y on their mobile

The world is going mobile, if it isn't already! That's what we keep hearing and that's because it's true. More and more people are checking their social media profiles, emails and performing other activities regularly over their mobile phones or tablets, and Google now penalises websites in search results if they are not mobile friendly.

There are plenty of companies out there who can create an app for you, specific to your requirements and at a price.

There are also drag and drop apps that allow you to create your own app or to convert your website into one.

Here is another great idea! Use a company such as COMO to convert your Facebook page into an app!

Using an app to market to your audience means that they can receive notifications on their phone about special offers you are running and when they use the app, they focus only on your brand and not a newsfeed full of distractions, including your competitors updates!

You can even use the app for running your loyalty marketing, allowing users to receive a reward after visiting your gym, restaurant or shop 10 times.

There are alternatives out there, but here's the link to the company that I have used to create apps for customers: http://www.como.com/

133. Make your business card socially acceptable

Imagine you have just met face-to-face with an important potential customer and he or she is not ready to buy from you just yet. Staying in touch is important, and business cards can easily be lost.

If the details are not uploaded into a sales tracking system as part of the sales process, then the business card can effectively become redundant. However, including your Facebook, Twitter or LinkedIn details on your business card means that you can quickly connect online with the person you have met, and continue to build a relationship long after you have met up face-to-face.

Please note that we are not just talking about sticking social media logos on your business card. Many people just won't take the time to try and find you on social media, because it requires time searching.

You must include your social media addresses so that they can connect with you within seconds.

Putting the right social media details on your business card is a one-time activity that takes very little time – yet it can make a difference to your sales and marketing activities.

134. Import followers from other social media profiles

Social media platforms such as Pinterest and TikTok are fully aware that many people have a greater presence on Facebook and Twitter, and that's why they invite you to connect with your friends and followers on other platforms.

Adding existing followers to a new platform is a quick and easy way of growing followers on the new platform, as well as strengthening the relationship with those people that you have already started interacting with.

This is another activity that should take you less than 5 minutes to do – just once. Yet it will make a huge difference to your social media results.

135. Make your 'on the road travels' a social advert

If you or your workforce travel a lot for business, then having your brand on your vehicle can reach a lot of people for a relatively low cost.

If you use a van or truck, then you may already have your telephone number or website on the side of your vehicle to promote your services.

That's great, but there is only one slight problem. Have you ever seen a van with services you require and tried to remember the telephone number or the website? There are too many distractions on the road to remember a series of numbers in a telephone number.

Adding your social media profiles can be easier for your customers to remember and you can always promote your services further on social media by sending visitors back to your website time and time again with links in your posts.

Don't just use the logos and don't promote too many social media platforms, otherwise people are less likely to connect. You must include the URL - your Twitter handle for example.

136. Add social to your product deliveries

A great way to connect with existing customers (and get them wanting to buy from you again!) is to put a leaflet in the box with any deliveries you make of physical products.

The leaflet doesn't have to be purely focused on social media, but if it includes your social media profiles and a call to action inviting them to connect, then you are in with a chance of building a long-term relationship with the customer.

Include a strong call to action as well which could simply be to follow you for great tips and advice, or you could run a competition where people can Like you on Facebook for a chance to win.

137. Share a promotion via email

If you send regular emails to your audience, you can use this channel to let your readers know about the promotion you are doing on social media.

This has various benefits. It provides content that can be included in your email marketing as well as increasing the chances of your readers interacting with you.

Some of your readers may not be so active on email, and they may never have thought about following you on social media (or never had a strong enough incentive to).

Once they have been informed of the promotion, they may well take a keener interest in your activities on social media.

On social media, it can be quite easy to miss the promotion that has been posted. Emailing people acts as a backup to make sure that your audience is aware, and ready to join in.

You may also want to send an email teaser telling followers to watch out for the promotion on social media.

Chapter 21: Analyse and improve

There is a saying "if you always do what you've always done, you will always get what you've always got" - and this applies to marketing.

If something is not working in your social media strategy, just increasing the volume of activity is unlikely to yield any better returns. In fact, it will take up a considerable amount of time and resource which could be better spent elsewhere.

Here are some ideas of how to analyse your activities so that you can make changes accordingly:

138. Use the analytics tools available

There are a huge number of online tools available that provide reporting on your activities on social media. Some are free and some can be quite costly.

Whatever tool you decide to use, at the very least take a good look at the analytics features those the various social media platforms such as Twitter or Facebook offer.

Twitter for example has vastly improved the analytics it provides and shows some great information on how many people have interacted with your posts. Just by seeing which posts got the highest visibility or retweets you will be able to identify what type of posts appeal most to your target market.

If the use of certain hashtags for example get a lot of attention, then you know to use those hashtags again in the future.

Facebook equally shows you how many people are seeing your posts as well as how your page Likes are growing over time. The information on demographics also helps you to understand if you are talking to the right target market.

If you are running an ads campaign, then the analytics tools on Twitter and Facebook are crucial. It can make the difference between cutting your spending if the analysis shows no results and increasing or doubling what you spend.

As an immediate action, why not spend 10-15 minutes reviewing one of your social media profiles to see what activity has worked and how you are progressing on social media.

If you are having problems interpreting the results, it's worthwhile engaging with a social media expert to analyse and review what is working and see how you can improve results.

139. Split Test

This is a great marketing expression... and a great way to make your marketing more effective. Split testing is about running two or more campaigns side-by-side to see what gets the best results.

If you have written a blog post, you may want to post your article on social media several times over a period of time using different wording.

Try this, and then go back and see what posts get the better results. As well as using different wording, try a different picture and on where relevant use different hashtags.

Images with a more human element to them are more likely to be interacted with while using hashtags that people search for conversations on will also increase your exposure. It's valuable information me saying this but you need to find which pictures and which hashtags work best for your line of business.

When analysing the results, you need to bear in mind other factors may have had an influence such as the time or the day of the post.

Split testing is especially useful when running ads or promotions. By running several versions of the same ad, you can see which ad gets the better results.

140. Use UTM Tracking

UT... What? With the world full of abbreviations here is another one! UTM (or Urchin Tracking Module) is a method of adding information at the end of a web link to track where a web visitor has come from – and what they do once they have clicked on your link.

Now that should make perfect sense! If not, don't worry about the abbreviation UTM and what it stands for, just bear in mind that it is more characters and letters at the end of a web link that is used for tracking results.

Whenever you see a web link that has "?" followed by some strange letters and words then this is likely to be UTM tracking. Here is a very basic example:

www.quotini.co.uk/?utm_source=Twitter&utm_medium=cpc&utm_campaign=Social%20tracking

At the end of the normal link for my home page (www.quotini.co.uk/), you will see the "?". This is where the UTM tracking code is placed. This tells Google that visitors to the homepage have come from Twitter (the source since utm_source=Twitter) and via a cost per click campaign (the medium since utm_medium=cpc). The campaign name is social tracking.

Using Google analytics, you can then understand better what marketing campaigns are working best.

I'm not going to go through the exact details of how the coding works but suffice to say that when you post a link on social media, if you add UTM tracking at the end of your link then you'll be able to know where visitors are coming from using Google Analytics.

For more information on UTM tracking, it's best to search for in Google for "UTM tracking". You can also search for "UTM builder" to see possible apps that can help you to create a link with UTM included in it.

If you are running a promotion, think carefully about how you want to track the results (we are assuming that you want to track the results – and you should!).

You could for example set up a different code for different social media channels. These codes entitle the purchaser to something of value.

If you are going to give away a free accessory or complimentary item with the main product when purchased, then make sure you can track it with a promotion code that they must use.

If they don't use the code then they don't get the free item, and you can't track if the campaign worked or not.

A TikTok exclusive code that is promoted purely through TikTok means you will know how successful or not a campaign has been as a result of using TikTok.

If you run a Facebook Ads or LinkedIn campaign, then use a code specific only to this campaign.

If your average monthly sales are 1,000 items but as the result of a Facebook and TikTok campaign your sales increase to 1,200 items, it's important to know where the results come from. Was it Facebook or TikTok (or neither!)?

Knowing that 180 people used the Facebook voucher code but only 20 people used the TikTok code clearly shows that Facebook was more successful. You can then use this data to plan your next campaign.

142. Set up telephone tracking numbers

Setting up telephone tracking numbers is a bit like setting up promo codes... but for telephones!

If you use a different telephone number for different marketing campaigns, then you can track how effective these campaigns are individually in converting activity into inbound enquiries.

This doesn't just apply to social media. You may run a local advert in a newspaper with a unique telephone tracking number. When somebody calls that number, it still goes through to your office but the only difference to your normal number is that you can track how many people dialled that number.

Because the tracking number is unique, you can analyse and understand exactly where the enquiries are coming from.

If your call log shows that most of your calls come from a magazine advert or social media campaign, then you know which source is generating leads.

Setting up tracking numbers is relatively quick and cheaper than you may think.

For a relatively low cost, you can now track where enquiries are coming from to understand where to spend your hard-earned marketing budget in the future.

143. Analyse your competition

Sometimes with marketing we just do not know how effective something is going to be until we try it, and this can take time. Just by analysing the social media profiles and marketing campaigns of your competitor you will be able to quickly see what seems to be working and what isn't.

It may be that your main competitor is on Instagram but not on Pinterest for example. If they are having a huge amount of success on Instagram the chances are it will work for you as well.

If, however, they have had very little success and not posted for a while then you may decide the opposite.

Note however that analysing your competition is a good starting point to generate ideas which may mean doing something different to your competition.

It may be that the poor success of one of your competitors on Pinterest is a result of them not applying their strategy correctly and you may be able to have greater success. Their failure may be an opportunity where you can succeed.

You should also analyse the content they are posting to see what is working and getting interactions. For example, if certain posts are getting high visibility and interactions then you might be able to replicate this success so that it can work for you.

A full analysis or a quick comparison?

If you don't have time right now for a full analysis then spend 5-10 minutes reviewing the profiles of your competitors to see what is getting the most interactions, understand what is working and decide if you can do similar – or better – campaigns. Consider:

- What has got people talking?
- Which platforms are they having most success on?
- Where are they sourcing content from and what topics are they covering?
- What hashtags are they using if any?
- What promotions have they run and is there any sign of success?
- Anything you didn't like and how would you have done it better?

If your competitor is having great success, then you have a benchmark to measure yourself against.

If, however, their attempts look poor and are under achieving then perfect! This is your chance to shine and take the lead. They are most probably missing a great opportunity and it's time to take advantage and get ahead.

When posting on social media, many scheduling tools allow you to shorten the URL. Shortening the URL also allows you to track how many people are clicking on the link.

It's worth using these tools to track what people are clicking on and what they are not clicking on. Try to include links in your posts as much as possible. There may be times when this is not appropriate or relevant to the content you are posting but having links in posts will help with marketing activity.

Having links in posts not only encourages interactions by enticing people to want to click on a link that they see but it also adds an extra element that you can track and measure.

For example, if you do a post about a product that you offer and include a link to the relevant page on your website then you can track the number of clicks as well as having increased the chances of selling the product by driving visitors to your website.

It also adds value to your fans as they can click on the link to find out more information on what you have posted about.

A popular comment I have received from new clients is that in the past they have tried social media but not got enough visitors to their site. The obvious place to start is by including links in posts!

If you want to find out more about what your followers and target audience would like to see you posting on social media, then why not conduct a survey to find out?

It will help you fine tune what you do and may give you some ideas that you hadn't thought of.

Conducting a survey also increases the interactions with your audience so that they can get more involved with you and your brand.

You can also increase the effectiveness of your survey by offering a prize draw so that there is a chance to win. Remember also to promote the survey through various channels and consider a Facebook subpage where people can complete the survey as well.

Facebook used to offer the ability to do polls on your Facebook page, then they removed the feature, then it came back, then it re-launched and, at the time of writing this, polls seem to only be allowed in Facebook Groups or when posting on your personal newsfeed.

This is probably already out of date but whatever the situation, there are other platforms that you can use to do polls.

LinkedIn and Twitter allow you to launch a poll which followers and connections can quickly and easily vote on their preferred option. This is a great tool to use although it does have a limitation that the votes are anonymous and can only be a single question.

Instagram allows you to do polls by creating a story (and my apologies if this has changed already!). This means that the results will disappear when the story expires so if you want to share the results, make sure to create a post in your newsfeed.

146. Measure Total Reach

There are lots of ways to measure your social media effectiveness and we won't go into the pros and cons of each here.

The ultimate measure is in sales growth, but this is not always easy as you can't always tell where a sale has come from.

One good indicator of how effective your campaigns are is how large your potential reach is (Total Reach) and how many people saw your post (Impressions).

The more your content gets shared, Retweeted or re-pinned then the more people are interacting with you, and the greater chance there is of people seeing your content – and your brand.

Different platforms use different terminology. Twitter, for example, focuses on Impressions which is how many times your post has appeared on someone's screen.

If 2 people – say Bob and Mary, see your post but Mary sees it on her phone and then sees it again later, either on the same device or her desktop, then that's a reach of 2 (i.e., two people have been reached) but the figure for impressions will be 3 since Mary has seen it twice. Impressions will typically be higher than reach.

You can look at both reach and impressions, but you might find that looking at reach is better as it's the actual number of people that have seen a post.

Having 1,000 impressions might sound good, until I tell you that the post reached the same person a thousand times, so the reach is 1! This might seem a bit extreme, but you get the idea.

If you get spikes or drops in your total reach, then try to understand why and see what you can do more of (and less of!) to be more successful.

There are various reporting tools that can help you understand your reach. Platforms such as Twitter and Facebook also do a great job of providing this information as well.

147. Repeat what campaigns and posts work

There is often a tendency to be over analytical – or be paralysed by them and not know what to do!

The important thing is to come to a conclusion as to what the next actions are and decide what has been learned from any analysis.

If specific campaigns and posts have had success, then repeat them – and continue to repeat them so long as they keep working. Of course, this also means dropping any activities that have been a complete flop and not worked.

Chapter 22: Sharpening the saw

If you have read 7 Habits of Highly Effective People by Stephen Covey, then you will be aware that I have taken the title of this chapter from his 7th habit.

I've done this because it's such an important habit in life and in marketing, and it's highly appropriate to social media marketing.

Why? (And what is Sharpening the saw)?

Sharpening the saw is about sharpening our skills and continuing to improve. Social media moves so fast that it's hard even for marketing professionals to stay up to date!

I once did a presentation on Facebook Ads, only to find that the user interface had changed overnight – and because of that, it was full of glitches.

Imagine trying to demonstrate your expertise while struggling to understand how to do what you are supposed to know!

Below are some tips for staying up to date with social media and the different ways that you can use it to grow your presence.

148. Take a course

There are plenty of marketing courses available online that are relatively low cost and great value for money.

These courses can really help to learn some nuggets of wisdom that you can use in your marketing.

I offer various courses and if you are looking for inspiration, feel free to email me for advice.

When signing up for a course, try to find one that's interactive. This will allow you to ask questions specific to you as well as to hear what other issues students bring up.

Face to face training is much better at this, although there are still online courses you can join that allow you to interact with students and the course teacher.

149. Join a forum

Alternatively, joining a forum or mastermind group that discusses marketing is a great way to share experiences and anything that's new.

I'm a great fan of mastermind groups as they really help business owners to share and support each other on a range of business issues.

A great way to develop your skills is to learn from the experts. If you use a professional digital marketing agency or work with someone closely that is passionate about social media marketing, then they will give you tips based on what's trending.

Outsourcing can allow you to focus on other activities while leaving social media marketing to the experts, so this can be a great long-term solution.

It can also, however, be a great short-term solution to learn from an expert if you are a start up business or you are just getting started on social media.

Chapter 23: Conclusion

*Companies and managers that find a way to harness social
media stand to gain.*
~ Ryan Holmes

Social media is a constantly changing landscape, and it can
be a full-time job staying up to date with the various tools
and trends as well as managing your activities.

When putting together your strategy and managing daily
activities always be sure to ask yourself "Is what I am doing
adding value to the business and helping to hit our
objectives".

Make sure to review your plans and activities regularly. The
way people engage and interact is changing so quickly that
even if you think you have a winning formula today, it may
not be the case tomorrow.

Even while writing this book, I have found the need to make
modifications based on new tools and changes to the
guidelines of social media platforms such as Instagram.

If you have found there is too much information in this book
to digest, read through it again or refer only to the relevant
sections when necessary.

If you are having changes made to your website, then refer to Chapter 3 to make sure you have the right social media elements included. If you are putting together content and need some inspiration, refer to Chapter 4 and 5 on content and so on.

Please do also check out my latest blog posts at https://www.thinktwicemarketing.com/blog and follow me on social media to stay up to date on the latest social media news.

I truly hope you have found the 150 top tips in this book of use and remember to keep it close as a reference guide for future strategy reviews – or simply for times when you need some inspiration.

I would love to hear your feedback about this book, so feel free to email me personally with feedback or with any questions about the various elements in this book.

My email address is Darren@thinktwicemarketing.com.

Thank you for reading and as a small token of appreciation I have included a free bonus section with some extras that are exclusive to readers of this book, to make sure that reading this book is just the start of successful social media marketing for your brand.

Thanks again – and I wish you all the best success on social media.

Chapter 24: Bonus Materials!

As an added bonus, I have included the following:

Additional ways to make your social media effective
5 Things you should NOT do on social media
A FREE 5-day Social Media Training course
A page of special offers on my website

The FREE 5-day Social Media Training course is delivered by email (one each day) and you can sign up for free on my offers page which is exclusive to readers of this book.

To take advantage of the free training course or special offers, use the link below:

https://www.thinktwicemarketing.com/book_offers

Additional ways to make your social media effective

Because social media is evolving so fat, I have updated this book a number of times since I wrote it in 2015.

This has meant adding and removing some of the 150 tactics and while some that I have removed no longer fit in within the structure of the book, some of them are still useful.

This section includes some of those tactics that might still be useful for your business.

151: Pay Per Click Ads

As social media grows, the effectiveness of Pay Per Click ads has grown in importance as it offers the ability to reach a large target audience relatively quickly.

Unfortunately, whereas using social media is free to use (it just takes up time and yes, you could argue that time is money!) the use of Pay Per Click ads does incur a cost.

It's important therefore to make sure that you measure what you're doing and try to understand what is working and what isn't.

If you understand what is working, make sure to repeat it. If you spend £100/$100 on Ads campaigns and it brings in a 200% return then the logical move is to repeat what worked and spend more, not less.

Connect Instagram to your business page, and Ads

When advertising on Facebook, you can have your ads appear on Instagram. These ads will show up as coming from your Instagram profile.

There are some great advantages to doing this. Firstly, Instagram does not allow standards posts to be clickable, but ads can be clicked on to take people to your website or landing page.

This also means that your ads offer something different to your target audience. Another great advantage is that there are more interactions on Instagram currently then any other platform, meaning the chances of potential customers clicking on your ad are greater.

To advertise on Instagram from a Facebook Ads campaign, you must have a business profile on Instagram, and you must have it linked to your Facebook page.

Focus on pay per click rather than impressions

When advertising you can pay based on how many people see your advert (impressions) or based on how many people click on the call to action.

Paying based on impressions is great for raising awareness of your brand but it has a major drawback. What if you set the wrong target audience or your ad copy isn't very good?

Thousands of people who aren't relevant could see your ad, or if they are relevant, they might see it but not be enticed to click on it because it's badly written.

I'm not saying you would create a badly created ad but there are always ways to make ads more effective.

When you pay based on impressions, you could be wasting money. If, however, you pay based on clicks then you can be more effective.

If nobody clicks on your ad, it could be because they aren't interested, or your ad isn't interesting.

And the good news is that you haven't wasted any money – and you can make changes to your ad to see if it gets a better response.

152. Keyword load your videos on YouTube

YouTube is a popular social media platform for people to search on, and many people search on YouTube to find out how to do things or to give them inspirational ideas (how to cook a particular type of dish for example).

How relevant the video is for YouTube to return it in search results is mostly based on what has been written in the title, description and how the video is tagged.

In other words, a brilliant video that meets your customers' requirements will not show up if you don't use the right keywords in the title and description.

Don't just post a video up and leave it at that. Make sure to give a full description including keywords that your customers may search for.

153. Create a content feed and Google Alert for content ideas

There are various tools you can use to aggregate the latest news for posting out on social media. If you specialise in helping businesses to trade internationally then you can use keywords in a content feed (such as Google Alerts) with the words "export" or "international trade".

You can also add certain blog sites to a content feed that will send you a notification when a new blog is posted. You can then share these blogs on social media if they are useful and relevant to your market.

I use Feedly as well as Google Alerts which sends me a daily or weekly email to my inbox full of lovely content that I can share.

It not only saves me time researching but also acts as a reminder to make sure I am posting fresh content every week. Another great tool that is free is Blogtrottr.

Here are the links:

www.blogtrottr.com
www.feedly.com
www.google.com/alerts or www.google.co.uk/alerts

Setting up an alert or feed takes less than five minutes and browsing through an email and posting one or two posts can take as little as five minutes a day (especially if you use a tool such as the Hootsuite widget mentioned earlier).

154. Post a video

Posing videos can be as tricky (or even trickier) as visual images. What do I post? How do I post it? How do I get make sure it is a great video? These are good questions and concerns.

You can spend a lot of money doing videos professionally as well as a lot of time, but as more and more people are now posting videos there has been a rise in the number of apps to make it easier.

YouTube tends to be the preferred platform for many reasons and Facebook has made great advances in the way you can post and share videos but there are some other interesting tools such as Vine, Instagram and Hyperlapse which help you to put together some interesting videos!

Instagram allows you to post pictures from your phone as well as videos. They also have a second app called Hyperlapse which is worth looking at. It improves the quality of the video you take with its built-in stabilisation feature and allows you to create videos that are played back at faster speeds.

Top tip: Get more reach on Facebook by directly uploading a video! Facebook wants its users to stay on Facebook and will always give a higher priority to videos that are uploaded to Facebook versus social media posts that include a link that takes them to YouTube!

When it comes to uploading videos to social media platforms, bear in mind the following limits:

Twitter: Videos must be less than 2 minutes, 20 seconds long
Instagram: Videos must be more than 3 seconds and less than 10 minutes.
LinkedIn: Videos can be up to 10 minutes in length and cannot be scheduled using a third-party app.
TikTok: The limit is 10 minutes
Facebook: Videos can be up to 240 minutes in length, and they can be scheduled through Facebook or a third-party app.

Although this might change, Facebook, Instagram and LinkedIn do not accept Gifs whereas Twitter does.

If you are looking at posting a video on social media, then I recommend checking to see if any of the above has changed.

155. Do a User Generated Content (UGC) campaign

A user generated content campaign is where you cleverly encourage or entice people on social media to effectively do a great post about your brand and product that other people on social media can see. You can also share this content, allowing you to fill your newsfeed with content that has been generated by the user (I guess the term user generated content is pretty self-explanatory!).

A good example of this might be to do a campaign asking people to give testimonials or post images of your product on Instagram using a particular hashtag. You give them a defined period of time over which they have to do this and at the end of the period, somebody will win a prize, which could be one of your products or a discount voucher towards their next purchase from you.

156. Add words to an image and post about your blog

Social media is a great way to drive people to your website or blog. One way to really make the post on social media more effective is by doing a visual post that blends an image with wording – especially on Pinterest!

If, for example, you have written a blog with tips on how to make house moving easier then source an image where someone is struggling to carry boxes or looking confused in a room with boxes all around them. Then, quickly and easily using some image editing software, overlay the words of your blog title, or a shortened version if it is too long.

This may sound like a lot of hard work but sourcing an image and then overlaying your blog title shouldn't take more than 20 minutes in total and will make a huge difference to the results of your post.

156. Use someecards.com for some light-hearted content

This website www.someecards.com allows you to take existing (and amusing) card templates and add your own words. These visual posts take very little time to put together and are a great way to make sure your content is not too serious, too often.

Make sure to read and comply with their terms and conditions on what can and cannot be posted for commercial use.

157. Use Facebook Ads to gain Likes

Okay I have to admit I'm not a great fan of using this over a sustained period of time. If you're going to use Facebook ads and spend money, then a wiser way of spending it is certainly on attracting potential customers that you drive directly to your online store or website.

Having said that, if you have just set up a Facebook page then you truly have a Catch-22 issue to solve with your lonely 'unliked' page. You only have two Likes, and nobody wants to Like a page with only two Likes so - what you do?

The first thing to do is post some great content. This may well be to an exceptionally small audience, but at least for people who visit your page it will encourage them to want to like your page so they can see future great content as well.

The next stage is to run a Facebook Ads campaign to your target market to grow your Likes up to a reasonable number.

You may want to include a strong call to action or promotion as well to give an even more powerful reason to Like your page. As you grow the number of Likes and interactions then it will become easier to grow your Facebook page in the future.

Once you have gained a reasonable number of Likes, re-evaluate, and reconsider the value of running a Facebook Ads campaign with this objective. I am not saying don't do Facebook Ads, just make sure you're spending your money wisely to grow your business and sales, rather than gain extra Likes.

158. Get Reviews on social media

Getting reviews on any platform (providing they are positive) is a powerful thing to have but even more powerful on LinkedIn and Facebook.

Platforms such as LinkedIn and Facebook love videos. If you have videos, then make sure to have them embedded on your profiles for people to see. It's a great way to make your profiles stand out, and it's proven to increase conversions of enquiries.

That's it in terms of what you should do. I hope you have found it useful.

I have talked a lot about what to do, but here are some bonus bullet points on things that you should NOT do on social media.

5 Things you should NOT do on social media

    1.   Do not link Facebook posts to your Twitter account

This is a big "NO-NO". I have seen this done so many times and it looks bad. An example I was involved in was when a contact I know posted wording a bit like the following on Facebook:

Wow! What a great networking event last night at our local venue, The Swan Inn, I really can't recommend the service and staff enough. They were absolutely amazing. Thanks everyone.

(Note: wording is not exact, and the location above is fictional to protect the person who wrote it).

Unfortunately, the post on Twitter was cut off to meet the character limit (which at the time was 140 characters) and it looked something like this:

Wow! What a great networking event last night at our local venue, The Swan Inn, I really can't recommend the service fb.com/LINK

Ouch! That does not look good! The post on Twitter looked to their 2,000 followers as though the location mentioned was being criticised, when in fact the post was meant to praise them!

Added to this, consider that not everyone on Twitter wants to use Facebook and if they read the post on their mobile phones then it is clunky having to click through to Facebook to read the rest of the post.

Doing this also excludes images so your feed on Twitter will just have a list of posts that are chopped and show a link. It doesn't look exciting or engaging in anyway.

2. Don't ignore complaints and unhappy customers

A great marketing strategy well executed can quickly unravel if bad publicity and a single bad customer experience goes viral. Always set a target to respond within 24 hours to a complaint by a customer. If you respond quickly and with a well worded response, then you can turn it into something positive.

An unhappy customer who did not get a delivery on time because of a logistics issue (possibly out of your control) may now be delighted, and other people on social media will see how professional and caring you are.

No matter how perfect we try to be, problems with customer experience do happen. The important success factor is how well you deal with those complaints.

3.   Do not use images illegally

It's always tough trying to find the right images – I'm sure I have said that a few times in this book! But, whatever you do, don't go stealing or using other people's images without their permission, and make sure you are using images legally.

Social media is free to use. Avoiding legal or copyright fines is the best way to keep it free and to avoid any lawsuits or heavy royalty fees.

I'm also convinced that there are companies out there who try to catch you out and are monitoring content online to see who they can make a quick buck on by threatening a lawsuit if you don't pay high royalty fees.

4. Don't just post promotional posts

People want to be social on social media, and also want to follow you because your posts add value to them. If all you do is post promotional content then over time, most fans are going to say to themselves "yes, ok, I get what you sell. You keep going on about it, and I'm not interested, I will just unfollow. I can visit your website if I want your product. I don't need to follow your profile on social media to keep being told about your products".

The aim of your content is to get people to like you as a business, and to associate themselves with your brand. Continual promotional posts will not give people the chance to want to know you further.

5. Don't take your foot off the pedal

Social media is ongoing. Don't just post 20 posts on Facebook in one week and then do nothing for 6 months. Content and activity need to be progressive, and not posting content for a period of time means that when you start again you really do have to... start again.

In other words, the good relationships you are building up risk being forgotten, and when you start posting again, there is a high risk of people unfollowing or unliking your page as they are not used to seeing your presence on their newsfeed.

I fully recommend reading "Hooked: A guide to habit forming products" by Nir Eyal in which he talks about how the brain comes to accept using apps and social media through the creation of habits over time.

Based on this, if you take away that regular content and interaction then you are breaking any habits or familiarity customers may have with you.

If you absolutely must do less on social media, for whatever reason, then the recommendation is to spread out your posts and interact less frequently so as to maintain a presence. Doing less is better than doing nothing at all.

Thanks again for reading my book. If you have found it a great read and of benefit, please leave a review to help other people.

Wishing you all the best on social media!

-Darren